A 2024 Starting-Point Guide

Stuttgart, Germany

Including the Baden-Württemberg Area

Barry Sanders – writing as:

B G Preston

ISBN: 9798873541010

3rd Edition – Updated April 2024

Acknowledgements: The author greatly appreciates Sandra Sanders' contributions and guidance.

Photography & Maps: Photos and maps in the Starting-Point Guides are a mixture of those by the author and other sources such as Shutterstock. Adobe Media, Wikimedia, Google Earth and Google Maps. No photographs or maps in this work should be used without checking with the author first.

Stuttgart's Schlossplatz
An inviting plaza in central Stuttgart and great place to start your explorations.

CONTENTS

Preface & Some Travel Suggestions

This Starting-Point guide is intended for travelers who wish to really get to know a city/area and not just make it one quick stop on a tour through Germany or Europe. Oriented around the concept of using Stuttgart as a basecamp for area explorations, this handbook provides guidance on sights both in town and nearby with the goal of allowing you to have a comprehensive experience of this beautiful city and area.

Several beautiful castles are easy to reach from Stuttgart.

The central focus or "starting point" of this guide is the German city of Stuttgart which is situated in the southwest area of the country. Several notable locales within the Baden-Württemberg area (the state for which Stuttgart is the capital) are also covered.

This is not a complete guide to the entire southern or western regions of Germany. Such a guide would go beyond the suggested scope of staying in one town and having enjoyable day trips from there. The area covered here is for the most popular sights which can be reached by train or car in 90 minutes or less each way.

Itinerary Ideas & Suggested Plan: If your travel schedule allows plan to stay 2 to 4 nights in Stuttgart. This is an area with a wonderful variety of sights outside the town.

Several days are needed to gain even a moderate understanding of what the region/area has to offer. If possible, keep a day open toward the end of your visit to tour or revisit areas which you discover during your first days in the area.

One Day in Stuttgart: If you just have one full day in this city, consider focusing on central Stuttgart and not heading out of town. Also, it is unlikely that any rational person can visit all the major attractions in one day so consider one of the two approaches:

- Museums, Monuments and Strolling: Stuttgart has several noteworthy museums in or close to the center of town. Consider spending an enjoyable exploring these attractions. Also, most of the better shopping and restaurants are found close to these sites so it is easy to combine shopping with museum browsing here and it is all within walking distance. Check chapter 6 for a list of several of the city's major points of interest.

- Automotive Excellence: Two substantial auto museums are just a short tram or bus ride from central Stuttgart, Porsche and Mercedes. The museums are not near each other, but it is possible to combine the two for a comprehensive, auto-focused day. Chapter 7 provides more information on these excellent museums. Each of these museums will take several hours to adequately explore.

Visit the Tourist Office. The Stuttgart tourist office is con-
veniently located across the street from the main train station,
the Stuttgart HBF. There is also an office in Stuttgart's airport.

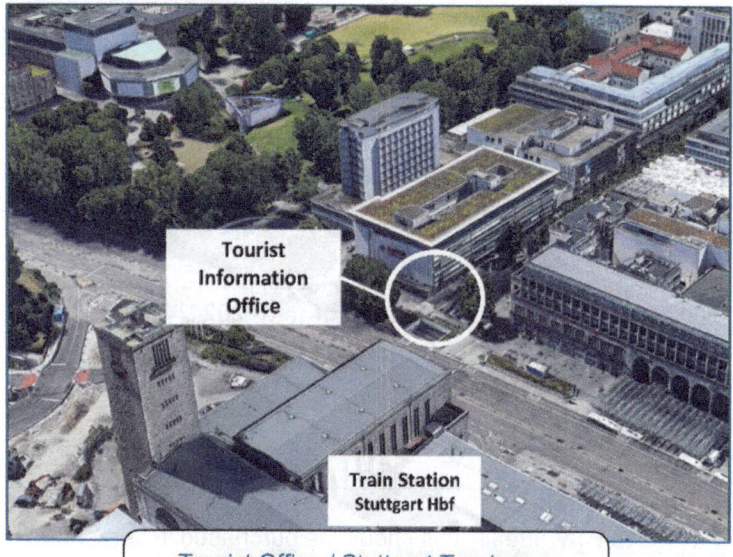

Tourist Information Office

Train Station
Stuttgart Hbf

Tourist Office / Stuttgart Tourismus
Across the street from the train station.

The personnel in this office (many speak English) can provide
current information on available tours and places to visit. Even
if you have done substantial research prior to your trip, it is likely
you will learn of additional opportunities which you had not previously uncovered.

Address: Königstraße 1A, 70173 Stuttgart (This is directly
across the street from the main train station and reachable by
an underground passage from the station.)

Stuttgart Tourist Office Website
www.Stuttgart-Tourist.de

Consider Acquiring a Stuttcard.
Stuttgart, like most cities, offers a local discount card. In Stuttgart, the card is known as a **Stuttcard** and provides a mixture of free entrances and discounts to local attractions and museums.

    There are variations on this card. The basic Stuttcard does not include transportation. The Stuttcard Plus does include local transportation plus several additional discounts. For example, With Stuttcard Plus, you receive free admission to the Porsche Museum which is not included in the basic card.

Stuttcard Cost as of mid- 2024[1]		
Duration	**Stuttcard**	**Stuttcard Plus**
24 Hour	24 €	34 €
48 Hour	30 €	403 €
72 Hour	35 €	53 €

Where to Buy: Ideally this should be purchased in person from the Tourist Office near the train station. Barring that, you may purchase it in advance from several sources, but it is advisable to purchase directly from the Tourist Office website which makes things easier if problems arise. That website is: **www.Stuttgart-Tourist.de.**

Important Timing Note: When you purchase one of these cards you must specify the day(s) it is to be valid. In some cities, these cards are valid from first use, but in Stuttgart, the cards are valid from the dates you select, even if you don't use it on those days. So, caution is warranted.

---

[1] **Price Disclaimer**: All prices cited in this guide are subject to change and are derived from public sources as of the time of this writing in mid-2024.

Obtain information on Local Transportation. Many European cities such as Stuttgart will have excellent tram and bus systems. In the case of Stuttgart, there is an expansive light-rail system which covers the city and much of the surrounding area. Understanding this system can be daunting at first so having a detailed map or app is helpful. The personnel in the Tourist Office can provide some assistance with this.

See chapter 5 for details on the area's transportation options and how to use them.

Stuttgart's U-Bahn and S-Bahn light rail system. An impressive network with many available routes.

Download Some Apps: With the incredible array of apps for Apple and Android devices, almost every detail you will need for a great trip is available up to and including where to find public toilets.

- VVS Mobil Stuttgart: Provided by Stuttgart transportation service. Details on bus and subway routes and area trains. Tickets may be purchased directly from this app.

- Stuttgart Taxi: A helpful app if you are likely to use area taxis at all.

- <u>Stuttgart City Guide</u>: Very complete app by MyCity, a firm which produces similar apps for other cities as well. Details area attractions, tours, dining and shopping. Highly recommended.[2]

- <u>Stuttgart Map and Walks</u>: This firm creates apps for numerous cities which detail suggested walks to discover the city along with detailed maps.

- <u>Stuttgart Travel & Explore</u>: Another well done app which details Stuttgart's attractions, dining and shopping opportunities.

- <u>The Fork</u> or <u>Open Table</u>: Worldwide, respected app detailing area restaurants. Dining reservations may be made directly from this app and ones like it.

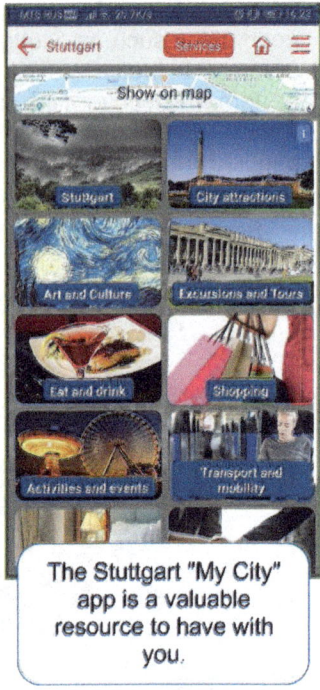

The Stuttgart "My City" app is a valuable resource to have with you.

- <u>Rome2Rio</u>: An excellent way to research all travel options including rental cars, trains, flying, ferries, and taxis. The app provides the ability to purchase tickets directly online.

- <u>Flush</u>: Easily find public restrooms/toilets when that need arises.

- <u>Trip Advisor</u>: Probably the best overall app for finding details on most hotels, restaurants, excursions, and attractions.

---

[2] **General Travel Apps**: There are numerous excellent travel apps to select from. The ones cited here are recommended by the author, but your search for helpful apps should not be limited to this.

1: Stuttgart Introduction

Stuttgart is appropriately thought of as a modern, cosmopolitan city. Major corporations such as Bosch, Mercedes, and Porsche are located here, and this helps build a dynamic and lively atmosphere.

The city itself has a population of only 630,000 people, but the metropolitan area has a population of over 5 million. It is the 6th largest city in Germany and the 4th largest metropolitan area. This is a large and vibrant city area but an easy one to navigate and get to know.

Schlossplatz / Palace Square
A central gathering place in the heart of Stuttgart.

Stuttgart's architecture is a mix of historical & modern structures.
Photo source: Wikimedia Commons

The city's name actually means *"Stud Garden"* which dates to the 10th century when this area was a prominent breeding ground for war horses. Some of this history is evident when you visit nearby palaces.

Stuttgart is the capital of the German state of Baden-Württemberg which borders France and Switzerland

Stuttgart is the capital of the German state of **Baden-Wurttemberg.** This large state borders France and

Switzerland. It offers visitors a wealth of experiences ranging from cosmopolitan Stuttgart, the Black Forest, numerous hiking and bike trails, wine routes, the resort town of Baden-Baden, and beautiful historic towns such as Heidelberg.

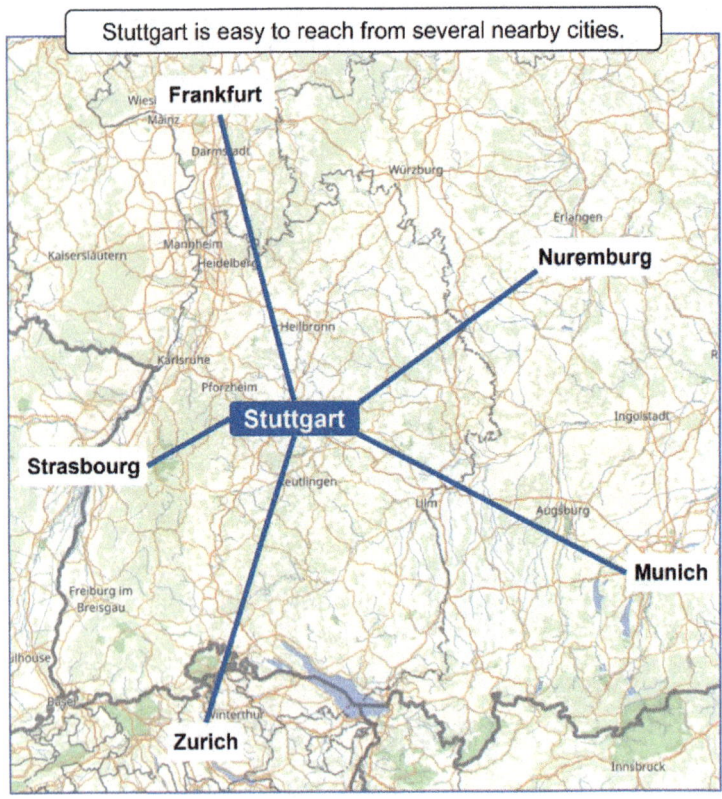

Stuttgart is easy to reach from several nearby cities.

This is an easy to reach city by train or plane with proximity to major cities such as Munich and Zurich. There are many cities and towns nearby which can be reached easily by train or car. You will find details on several suggested day trips in chapters 9 and 10.

What to Expect When Visiting Here: This is a city with a fresh and new feel. The central city area, often referred to as the **Inner City,** sits in a broad river valley surrounded by low hills. Stuttgart is divided into districts which fall into the two general classifications of "inner" and "outer." Visitors to this city will likely spend most time exploring the five inner districts with the "Mitte" district being the most central. The outer districts cover a range of rolling hills which provide an interesting topography to the area.

Konigstrasse - Stuttgart's most notable pedestrian shopping street which stretches for more than 1 km south from the train station.

One attribute of Stuttgart which quickly becomes apparent is the expansive green areas around the city. This is an area of mixed-use housing and green spaces. Surprisingly, in addition to forest and park land, there are many vineyards in the immediate area, and some are even visible from the city.

The central city area is fairly compact and measures approximately 2km in length and 1km in width. This section of town is largely in a grid with the train station at the northern end

for most activities and attractions. The central city area is characterized by shopping and is labeled as a shopper's paradise by many.

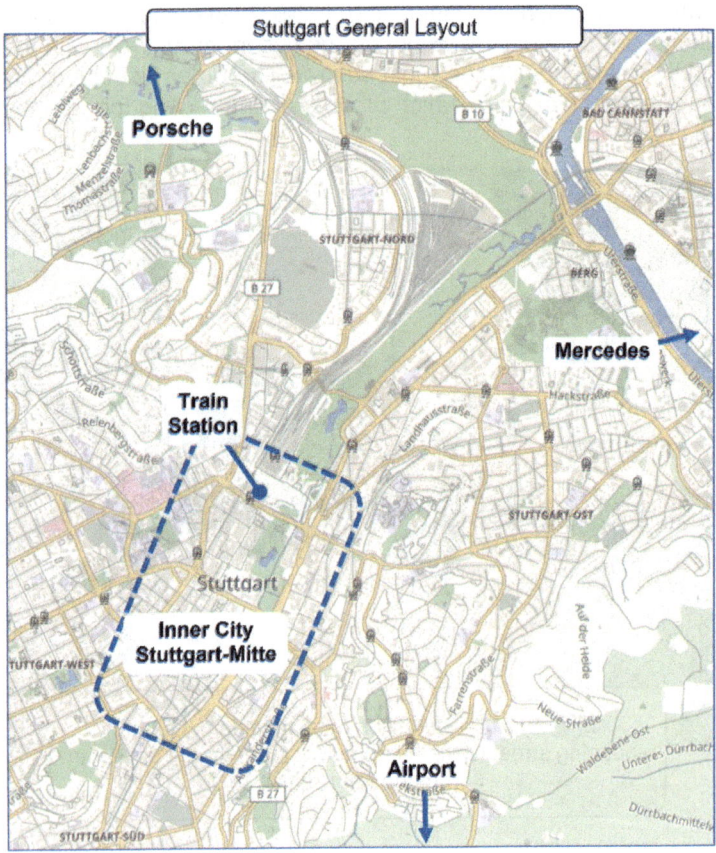

Major pedestrian shopping streets such as the Konigstrasse, (Königstraße) which stretches over 1km, offer every type of shopping imaginable. There is even an underground mall.

Views of Central Stuttgart

Bordering the central city district is one of the university areas which houses the **University of Stuttgart**. This university is home to approximately 24,000 fulltime students, about 1/3 are foreign. This contributes significantly to the youthful and cosmopolitan feel of the city.

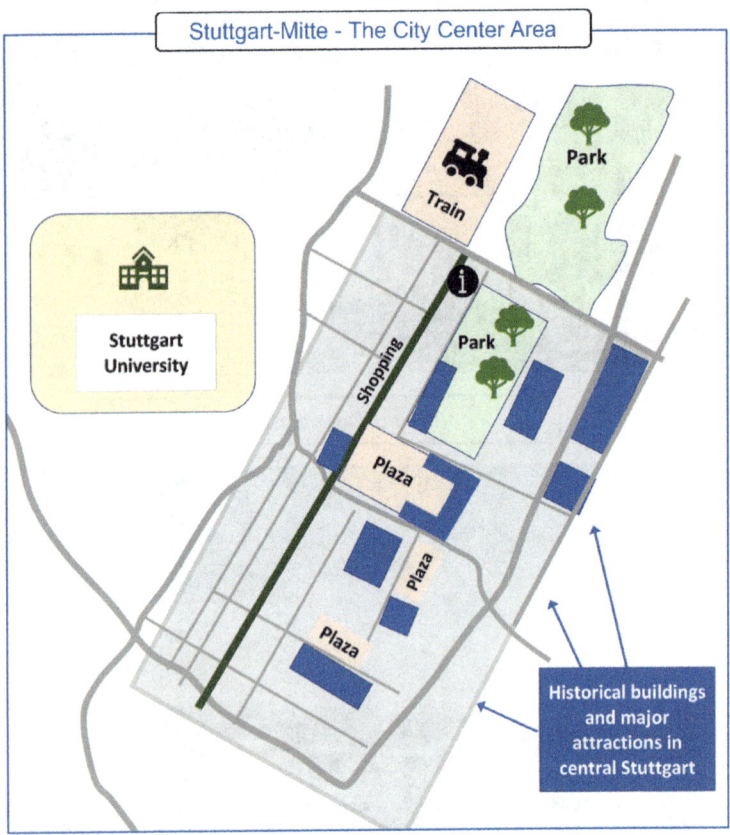

This is a great town for walking and the newer streets and walks are generally friendly to individuals with limited mobility. In addition to the shopping streets and pedestrian-friendly atmosphere, there are numerous parks. One very large park is the **Schlossgarten,** a long and narrow park which stretches from the train station all the way to the Neckar River. There are a number of interconnected parks here which stretch for eight kilometers. This is often referred to as the "Green U."

The hills bordering central Stuttgart include parks, trails and wine country which are easy to reach for walks or bike rides.

Stuttgart evolved as an agriculture area and the Neckar River played an important role in its local economy and development. Unlike many cities which are developed around a primary river, with Stuttgart, the river is not central to the town and is off to the eastern edge. Few attractions for tourists lie along this river with the notable exception of the Mercedes Museum.

There are several open, public areas which will draw your attention and make great starting points for your explorations. The most notable of these is the **Palace Square or Schlossplatz**. This is a large open park which has **the New Palace** (Neues Schloss) along the eastern edge and the **Old Palace**/Castle (Altes Schloss) on the square's southern side.

One other notable aspect of Stuttgart is the small number of historic buildings and minimal number of quaint lanes to stroll and explore. This is due largely to the substantial rebuild which was required at the end of WWII, which gives the city its modern feel.

Plan Around Closings:

To ensure your time in Stuttgart is not wasted, it is important to note the following:

Many shops are closed on Sunday.

Most museums are closed on Monday.

Some History: The history of Stuttgart and the Neckar Valley (the river valley in which Stuttgart sits) has documented history going to the 7th century BC, over 2,700 years ago. The valley's rich land enabled growth of agriculture and the cultivation of a wide range of crops. Like many cities in Europe, the Romans were an important part of the area's development.

Horses became an important aspect of the area's development. The breeding of war horses gave the area prominence in the 10th century.

Prior to WWII, the area had grown to be an important manufacturing area with automotive production being a key component. This, unfortunately, led the city to be a significant target of the Allies during the war.

The city was largely destroyed during WWII with over 50 bombing raids which leveled the majority of Stuttgart. In the aftermath of the war, the city was largely rebuilt under the Marshall Plan. As a result, this city does not have an expansive historic quarter as many cities do. In the rebuild, only a modest number of historic buildings were repaired with the focus on crafting a new, modern city.

Stuttgart was heavily bombed during WWII.
Photo source: Wikimedia Commons

One set of programs which occurred after WWII was for Allied nations to actively occupy Germany. While this has dramatically changed in size and scope, there are still over 10,000 U.S. troops stationed in the area across several facilities including the large "USAG Stuttgart."

Stuttgart has continued to grow and prosper since the war. Not only is the automotive industry strong, but other leading industries such as Aerospace and Information Technology are strong. This mix of growth industries has caused Stuttgart to be an attractive place to move for work This growth at first came from East Germany where job opportunities were poor and lately has become a popular destination to live for individuals worldwide. Today, over half of the local population does NOT have area ancestry.

A Few Fun Facts and Tidbits about Stuttgart:

- The Home of Gas-Powered Cars: We tend to think of Detroit as the focal point for automotive history but much of the automobile's history started here. In 1886 the first petrol powered car was invented here by Carl Benz and Gottlieb Diamler. The first car was a small three-wheel vehicle.

- A City of Culture: Stuttgart has been ranked by leading sources as Germany's leading city of culture. Visits to area shows, museums and cultural events proportionately exceeds all other German cities.

- A Haven for Sports Lovers: Stuttgart is an excellent place to experience professional sports.

Central Stuttgart

The Mercedes Benz Arena / MHP Arena
Consider viewing local Soccer at its best while here.
Photo source: Arne Muselef - Wikipedia

The city has been named as one of Europe's sports capitals. Soccer/Football is, not surprisingly, one of the leading sports here but you will also find baseball, basketball and hockey.

VfB Stuttgart, the local Soccer/Football organization is the fifth largest in Germany. Their games may be viewed in the 60,000 seat MPH Arena (Mercedes Benz Arena) which is adjacent to the Mercedes Benz headquarters and museum.

UEFA Euro
Stuttgart will be one of 10 German cities in July 2024 to host this major football tournament.

- Stuttgart and Automotive Excellence: Much of the area is defined by major industries such as Porsche and Mercedes-Benz. Even with this substantial industry, Stuttgart is a very green city. The large factories, such as the one for Mercedes-Benz, are on the edge of town and require a short commute to reach them

Mercedes-Benz has massive administration and production facilities in Stuttgart.
Photo source: Google Earth

- Wine has an integral role in Stuttgart: The Romans first brought grape vines to this area and, even today, you can find vineyards immediately on the town's outskirts with some vineyards within the city proper. The city of Stuttgart actually runs an area vineyard. Wines grown here lean toward sweater varieties such as Riesling.

Several wine trails for walking or biking are within walking distance of central Stuttgart. A map of the area's wine trails may be picked up in the Tourist Office.

Several wine trails, designed for walking or biking, are close to central Stuttgart.

- The Neckar River and Valley: Stuttgart is nestled in the Neckar Valley. Framing this valley and the city center is the Neckar River to the east and rolling hills which surround much of the city. Boat tours are available.

The Neckar River and vineyards just south of central Stuttgart.
Photo source: Berndt Fernow-Wikipedia

2: Traveling to Stuttgart

As an active center of business and industry, Stuttgart is well connected and is easy to reach by air or train.

The train station is right in town, requiring minimal extra travel once you arrive and the airport is less than 30 minutes south of town. The city's excellent transportation system connects directly to the terminals of the train and airport. The expansive system enables easy transfer to many areas in and neighboring central Stuttgart.

Arriving by Train: [3] The main train station, **Stuttgart Hbf** (Stuttgart Central Station), is a large terminal which is in the heart of town. The station houses several shops and restaurants which can be an added benefit to many. This is a very busy station so, for first-time visitors, consider adding in some time to learn the layout.

Train Station Website

The Stuttgart Hbf website provides excellent details on available services and detailed maps of the station's layout.

www.Bahnhof.de/Stuttgart-hbf

---

[3] **Train Station Upgrade and Expansion**: A massive improvement project is underway to completely modernize and expand Stuttgart's train station and much of the rail network. As of this writing, this large project is expected to continue to 2025, if not later. Expect to find work in progress with some construction areas when traveling through this terminal.

Connecting to this station are many local transit lines known as the U-Bahn and S-Bahn systems. Details on this system may be found in chapter 5 of this guide. The presence of the local light-rail systems at the station greatly adds to the ability to go almost anywhere in the town without hassle.

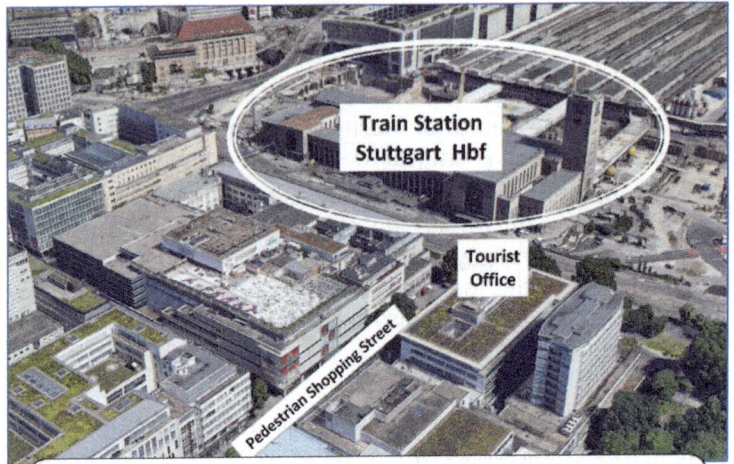

Stuttgart Train Station / Stuttgart Hauptbahnhof (Hbf)
Located in the center of the city.
Photo source: Google Earth

Across the street from the station is the **Stuttgart Tourist Office**. Taxis line up immediately outside the station, and during normal business hours, they will generally be available.

When exiting the station, you will encounter a busy street lined with modern buildings. If you do not have a specific destination in mind, such as a hotel, consider going across to **Königstrasse**. This impressive shopping area was the first pedestrian zone in Germany. Another option is to head underground to visit the shopping area which sits between the train station and Königstrasse.

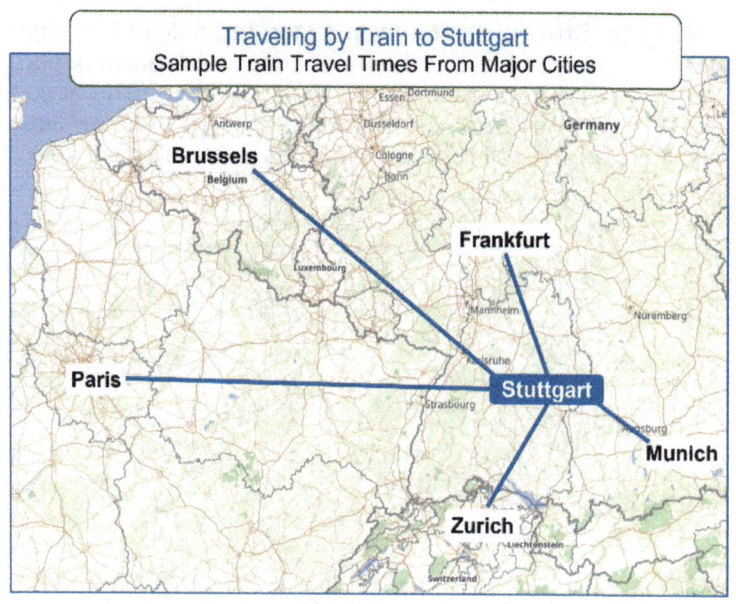

Traveling by Train to Stuttgart
Sample Train Travel Times From Major Cities

To/From	Typical Time	Trains Per Day
Brussels	4 Hours +	5 +
Frankfurt	1 Hr 20 Min +	15 +
Munich	2 Hr 15 Min +	10 +
Paris (City)	3 Hr 20 Min +	5 +
Zurich	3 Hr +	5 +

Flying to Stuttgart: The main airport in Stuttgart is a short distance south of the city. This is a busy international airport, the 6th biggest in passenger arrivals in Germany. The airport sits about 6 miles south of central Stuttgart (as the crow flies) and there are several convenient options for traveling into town.

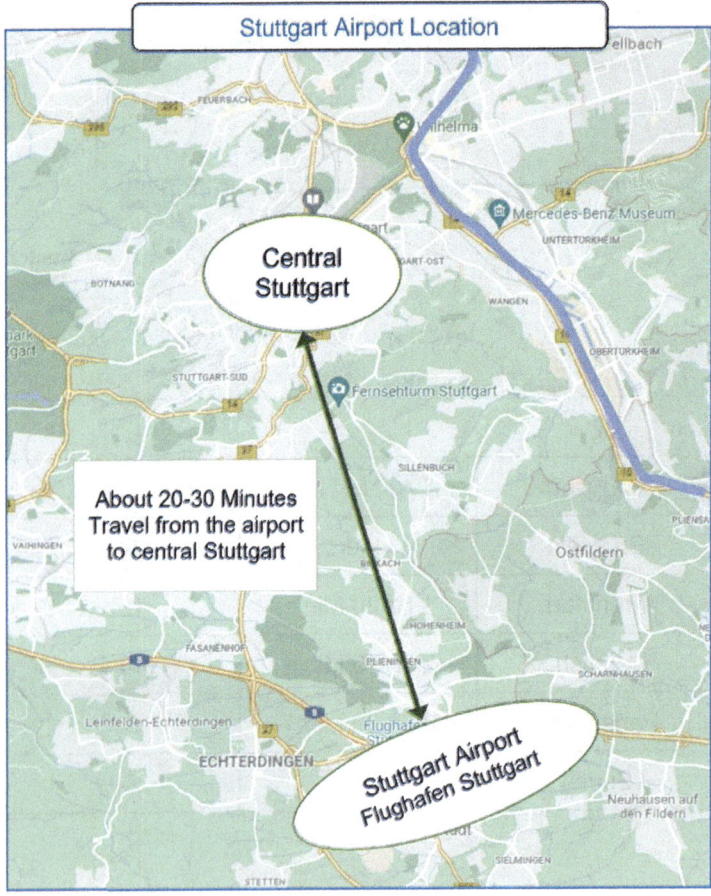

About 20-30 Minutes Travel from the airport to central Stuttgart

Travel time into town will be at least 20-minutes, even by car. Trains can take from 20 to 30 minutes, depending on the one selected.

If you choose to book lodging here instead of in town, there are two large hotels in the airport complex and numerous hotels in the small towns neighboring the airport. The hotels at the airport are: The Wyndam Stuttgart Airport and the Mövenpick Hotel Stuttgart Airport. Both are large 4-star hotels.

Interior of the Stuttgart Airport - Flughafen Stuttgart
Photo Source: Giftzwerg 88 - Wikimedia Commons

Light Rail into Town: Stuttgart's light rail / subway system services the airport, making this a convenient and affordable way to travel into the city or many of the neighboring towns. The train lines are easy to find and run under the main concourse. Watch for signs pointing to "S" train lines.

The routes into central Stuttgart are direct and do not require a change of train. These trains run approximately every 15 minutes during prime hours. Tickets must be

Look for the (S) signs in the airport to direct you to the subway.

purchased before boarding and validated when boarding. Ticket machines may be found both at luggage collection and in the train entry area. [4]

The transit system can be confusing at first as pricing is established by zones traveled, the distance you will travel. Even day tickets are priced by zones. If you are traveling into town, consider a purchase of 2 zones to ensure you are fully covered.

Stuttgart Airport Website

The airport website does provide helpful information such as ground transportation and airport services.

www.Stuttgart-Airport.com

Airport Taxi and Car Service: If your destination, such as a hotel, is in town but not close to Stuttgart's central station (Stuttgart Hbf), consider taking a taxi or one of several available transfer services which may be booked in advance. These services are more expensive than taking the train or bus (Likely over € 40 plus tip), but they offer the significant advantage of taking you directly to your lodging.

You can generally find available taxis and transfer services outside the baggage collection area without needing an advance reservation. If you prefer to ensure that a car will be waiting for you may book through one of the following:

• Hoffman Bus & Taxi

---

[4] **Tram and Subways into town from the airport**: The Stuttgart transportation network is a "good news / bad news" situation. On the positive site, you have multiple options. In addition to the S-Bahn cited in this chapter, the U-Bahn, which is the area's tram system, also departs from the airport and works its way into town – thus the bad news of several options which can be confusing. For first-time visitors, unless you are provided other guidance, consider just sticking with the U-Bahn option which takes you directly to the central station.

- www.Kurz-Aviation-Service.com – provides VIP limo and airport fast tracking service. (Expensive)
- www.AirportTaxis.com and select Stuttgart.

Direct Train from Frankfurt Airport: Due to the large number of international flights into Frankfurt, a popular route for many travelers into Stuttgart is to fly into Frankfurt and take the train from there.

Trains are available directly from Frankfurt airport into central Stuttgart and the trip takes around 2 hours. Numerous trains depart each day, and the cost is minimal, generally around €20-30 for a standard-class ticket.

In both cases of flying into Stuttgart or Frankfurt, a train into town will likely be needed. For added comfort, first-class seats are generally available.

3: When to Visit

Like most areas in Europe, your best times to visit this area are late Spring, early Summer, and Fall. This holds true especially if you wish to avoid crowds, enjoy touring, and want to get out into the country to explore the natural attractions.

Tourist Crowds: Stuttgart is not high on most lists of cities to visit in Germany. Cities such as Munich, Cologne, Berlin, and Frankfurt typically rate much higher. Most "Top 10" lists either do not include Stuttgart or keep it near the bottom of the list. This is actually a great aspect of this mid-size city as it is rarely overrun with tourist crowds and the attractions are more available to visit and explore.

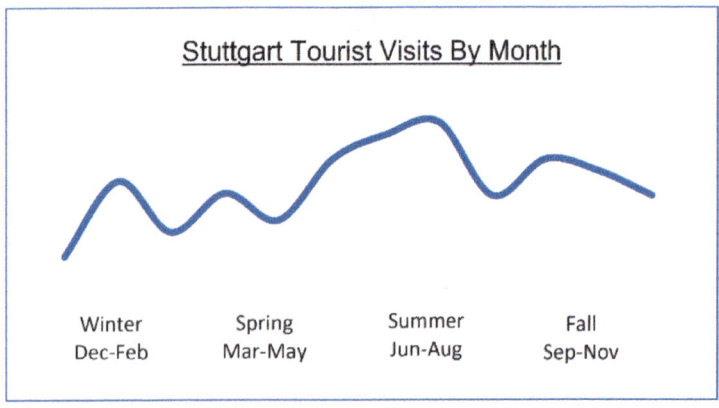

Stuttgart Tourist Visits By Month

| Winter | Spring | Summer | Fall |
| Dec-Feb | Mar-May | Jun-Aug | Sep-Nov |

There are several major events held each year in Stuttgart which can add to the crowding. These include the massive Stuttgart Beer Festival, the Christmas Market, and the "CMT" (the world's largest trade fair for tourism and leisure). In general, these events add an element of fun, rather than throngs of tourist groups crowding the museums. Details on several of the more popular events are discussed further in this chapter.

Local Climate: Stuttgart sits in a temperate climate zone and provides pleasurable weather for much of the year, even with temperatures varying significantly across the seasons

Light rain is common throughout the year, but the surrounding hills often act as a deterrent to strong storms. Overall rainfall during a typical year is around 28 inches. For comparison, Paris has 25 and London has 29 inches annually.

Winters tend to be cold but not excessively. Temperatures are generally slightly above freezing. Light winds from the west, the "Westerlies," often blow in the winter, adding to the pleasant feel of the area. Skies are often grey in the winter here and, given the nearby low mountains, snowfall is common, but it is generally light.

Stuttgart in the Spring can be Beautiful

In the summer, weather tends to be cool to warm with frequent light rains or thunderstorms. The city resides in a bowl surrounded by low hills and this topography mixed with urban development can create uncomfortable heat in the city center.

Average Stuttgart Climate by Month			
Month	Average High	Average Low	Avg Rain
Jan	39 F / 17 C	27 F / -3 C	1.6 inches
Feb	42 F / 5 C	27 F / -2 C	1.4 inches
Mar	50 F / 10 C	33 F / 1 C	1.9 inches
Apr	57 F / 14 C	39 F / 4 C	2 inches
May	66 F / 19 C	47 F / 8 C	3.4 inches
Jun	75 F / 24 C	53 F / 11 C	3.4 inches
Jul	79 F / 26 C	56 F / 13 C	3.4 inches
Aug	79 F / 26 C	55 F / 13 C	2.7 inches
Sep	67 F / 20 C	49 F / 2 C	2.3 inches
Oct	58 F / 14 C	42 F / 5 C	2.3 inches
Nov	47 F / 8 C	34 F / 1 C	2 inches
Dec	40 F / 4 C	29 F / -2 C	2 inches

Major Festivals and Events in Stuttgart: There are several popular events in and near Stuttgart each year. Visiting one of these can be a great addition to your visit. The only downsides are the added crowds in Stuttgart and increased lodging rates. Information on some of the leading events follows. (This is not a complete list of all events in Stuttgart).[5]

When	Event
January	CMT – Travel and RV Expo
Mid-Apr to Mid-May	Springfest
Late July	Stuttgart Jazz Open
Late Aug to early Sep	Stuttgart Wine Festival
Late Sep to early Oct	Beer Festival
Late Nov thru Dec	Christmas Market

CMT: Europe's largest show for travel and tourism with over 2,000 exhibits ranging from tours to RVs. In mid-January every year, this huge travel-related exhibit takes place at the large Messe-Stuttgart conference complex which is adjacent to the airport.

To travel to this conference, use the S-Bahn or other airport transport. The S-Bahn stops a short distance from the conference hall.

- Website: **www.Messe-Stuttgart.de/cmt**

---

[5] **Events in and near Stuttgart:** The area's tourist website, www.Stuttgart-Tourist.de provides updated details on most events, small and large held in and near Stuttgart.

The Travel and RV exhibits at the CMT are expansive and very popular.
Photo Source: CMT

Springfest. (Stuttgarter Fruelingsfest): This is the largest Spring event around Stuttgart in the and attracts over 1 million people. It is also the largest spring festival in Europe. Expect

to find several music groups, beer, carnival-type rides, more beer, and a very lively atmosphere.

Note: This festival is sometimes referenced by the term "Cannstatter Wasen" which is the location of the festival.

- Timing & Location: This fair normally runs from mid-April to the middle of May. In 2024 the dates are April 20 to May 12. It is held at the large open area "Cannstatter Wasen" which is along the Neckar River and close to the Mercedes-Benz Museum.

- Getting Here: Both the U-Bahn and S-Bahn stop here, but the S-Bahn station is closer. Get off at the Neckarpark stop.

- Website: www.Stuttgarter-Fruehlingsfest.de

Think Beer and lively Beer Halls- when attending the
Stuttgart Springfest.
Photo source: Stuttgarter-Fruehlingsfest.de

- - - - - -

The Springfest grounds sit alongside the Neckar
River and close to Mercedes stadium and museum.
Photo source: Zonk43-Wikimedia Commons

~ ~ ~ ~ ~

Jazz-Open Stuttgart:[6] If you enjoy jazz, this is the place to be in July each year. Running for 10 days in late July, this event brings in noted performers and is presented at several venues. The larger concerts occur in the open Schlossplatz in the center of town.

Tickets should be purchased in advance as the more popular artists sell out quickly. Caution: Festival passes can be quite expensive.

- When: July 18-29, 2024
- Website: www.JazzOpen.com

Sting performing at the Stuttgart Jazz Open
Photo Source: Stuttgarter-Fruehlingsfest.de

~ ~ ~ ~ ~

[6] **Crowd and Noise Caution**: The center of activities for this festival is in the heart of Stuttgart. This is good and bad. If you are in town for the festival, the location is very convenient. If you are here during this time as a normal visitor – you will find central Stuttgart to be very crowded and noisy, especially at night.

Stuttgart Wine Festival: (Often referred to as the Stuttgart Wine Village.) Stuttgart has a long history with wine which dates to Roman times and this history is celebrated by a large wine festival each Fall.

This event normally runs from the end of August and ends in early September. The central location for this event is at the MarktPlatz, a large square a few blocks south of Schlossplatz.

- **Website**: **www.Stuttgarter-Weindorf.de**

The Stuttgart Wine Festival - an active and fun event.
Photo source: Stuttgarter Weindorf

~ ~ ~ ~ ~

Stuttgart Beer Festival: This is the time to buy and wear your traditional German Swabian clothing.[7] Stuttgart does not have an official Oktoberfest as that honor is given to Munich. Instead, they put on a large Fall or Beer Festival called the Stuttgart Cannstatt.

This event is held in late September through early October and attracts over three million visitors. It is huge!

- Location: Held at the Cannstatter Wasen grounds which is adjacent to the Mercedes-Benz complex.

- Website: www.Cannstatter-Volksfest.de.

~ ~ ~ ~ ~

Christmas Market (Stuttgarter Weihnachtsmarkt): is one of Germany's most popular Christmas markets. There are over 300 booths each year along with numerous concerts and events for children. Come here in the evening to enjoy the city and market fully lit for the holiday.

- Location: The center of this large event is in the MarktPlatz which is a few blocks south of the Schlossplatz and the new palace.

- Timing: This market typically starts in the last week of November and runs through much of December. Exact dates and times for the upcoming 2024 festivities may be found on the festival website.

---

[7] **Swabian Wear** – It is acceptable to wear Dirndl and Lederhosen in Stuttgart although this is often considered to be more local to Bavaria. The official traditional wear for Stuttgart is termed "Swabian" which is similar for men in some regards to Bavarian wear with a Gypsy flair.

- **Website:** www.Stuttgarter-Weihnachtsmarkt.de

The Stuttgart Christmas Market is a lively event with
numerous food stalls, concerts and rides.
Photo source: Baden de - Wikimedia Commons

4: Where to Stay

Where you choose to stay when visiting a new city is essentially a personal choice. You may prefer hotels or rental apartments. Picking a place guided by your budget may be critical to you.

Regardless of the motives which drive your selection of accommodation type, the "where in town should I stay?" question is critical to helping you have an enjoyable visit.

This guide does not provide details on all hotels in Stuttgart. There are simply too many to describe. There are many fine and dynamic online sources such as Booking.com or Trip Advisor [8] which give far more detail than can be provided here. These sites will provide answers to every question about a property you are considering and allow you to make reservations once you have made your selection.

> **Author's Recommendation:**
>
> Stay in the heart of the city – the area known as Stuttgart Mitte.
>
>

---

[8] **Hotel Ratings:** All hotel ratings cited here are a blend from several sources such as personal experience, Booking.com and Trip Advisor as of mid-2024. Other sources may present different ratings. All ratings are subject to change. All lodging listed here fall into the categories of hotel or inns. No "AirBnB" type of lodgings are described.

Recommended Area: Quality lodging may be found throughout the area including Stuttgart's suburbs, the airport area, and neighboring towns. For first time visitors, unless you have a specific destination outside the city center, it is recommended that you **stay in the city center.** This guide only details selected hotels, but this area recommendation holds true for all lodging types such as Air B & B.

Consider selecting lodging in the area which lies between the train station to the north and Marktplatz to the south. This area stretches about 1.5 km in length. The noted Schlossplatz is in the center of this area with the MarktPlatz sitting near the southern boundary.

Benefits of staying here include:

- Proximity to the train station
- Numerous light-rail stations
- Major museums are here
- Most notable shopping areas are here
- Major centers of activity such as the Schlossplatz and Marktplatz.
- More restaurants and bars than you can count.

One huge exception to this recommended area is the airport. IF, and only if, you have an early departing flight or will be visiting one of the exhibits such as the Travel show at the airport's convention center, you may want to consider staying at one of the airport hotels.

Lodging to Consider: The map on the following page shows several hotels which are well rated and well located.

Each of these properties receive good ratings and offer visitors several amenities such as restaurants on site. They are also near public transportation.

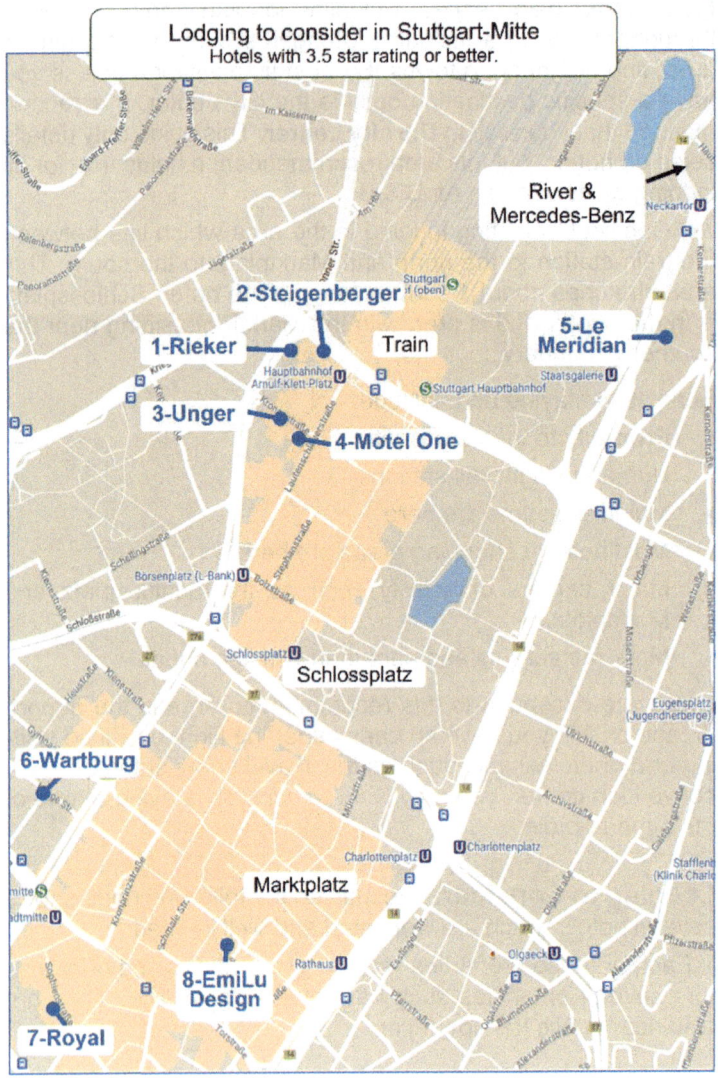

Lodging to consider in Stuttgart-Mitte
Hotels with 3.5 star rating or better.

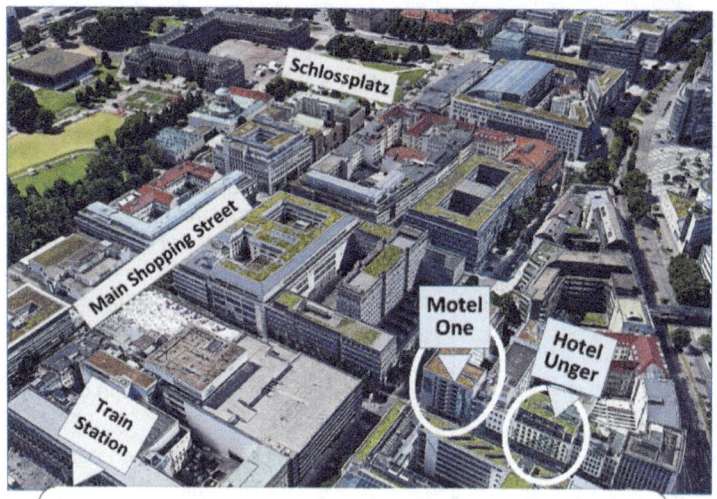

Several hotels such as the "Motel One" and "Hotel Unger"are in the heart of the city center.
Photo Source: Google Earth

Suggested Lodging in Central Stuttgart		
(All selected lodging has 3.5 or better rating)		
Hotel	**Address & Details**	**Rating**
1 Hotel Rieker am Hauptbahhof	Friedrichstraße 3 70174 Stuttgart Close to the train station. A casual, fairly modern property. Rooms are fairly small. Complete buffet breakfast available. Well kept, property. **www.HotelRieker.de**	3.5 stars
2 Steigenberger Graf Zeppelin	Amulf-Klett-Platz 7 70173 Stuttgart Across the street from the Stuttgart train station and immediately next to	4.5 stars

Suggested Lodging in Central Stuttgart

(All selected lodging has 3.5 or better rating)

	Hotel	Address & Details	Rating
	Steigenberger Graf Zeppelin	major shopping. There is a full array of restaurants and nightlife in the immediate area. About a 10-minute walk to the Schlossplatz, the central point within Stuttgart. Modern luxury with all desired facilities and conveniences including a fitness center, bar, and restaurant. Often listed as one of the best hotels in central Stuttgart **www.HRewards.com** - then search for Stuttgart.	
3	Hotel Unger Stuttgart	Kronenstraße 17 70173 Stuttgart One block south of the train station and in the heart of the major shopping area. A short walk to the Schlossplatz. Numerous restaurants are in the immediate area. Mid-size hotel with 130 rooms. Rooms are soundproof which helps as this is a busy area. Deemed to be somewhat "old style" by many reviewers. **www.Hotel-Unger.de**	4 stars
4	Motel Motel One Stuttgart-Mitte	Lautenschlagerstraße 14 70173 Stuttgart Author recommended. **www.Motel-One.com** Then search for Stuttgart. Note, there are several "Motel One" properties in Stuttgart.	4 stars

Suggested Lodging in Central Stuttgart

(All selected lodging has 3.5 or better rating)

	Hotel	Address & Details	Rating
5	Le Méridien Stuttgart (By Marriott)	Willy-Brandt-Straße 30 70173 Stuttgart Two blocks from Stuttgart Hbf train station and the shopping and facilities near the station. Across the street from the hotel is a large park, the Middle Schlossgarten. There is a limited number of restaurants and shops adjacent to the hotel, so a walk into the center is often needed. **www.Marriott.com** Then search for Stuttgart	4.5 stars
6	Wartburg Hotel	Lange Strasse 49 70174 Stuttgart Situated off to the south-western edge of the city's center, this property sits on a quiet side street. It is a short walk (2 or 3 blocks) to the center and to the popular MarktPlatz. **www.Hotel-Wartburg-Stuttgart.de**	3.5 stars
7	Hotel Royal & Restaurant	Sophienstraße 35 70178 Stuttgart This mid-size hotel is the furthest south of all properties listed here. Its biggest negative is the walking distance into the heart of town. There is a full-service restaurant on site and enjoyable pubs nearby. Contemporary vibe in the rooms and restaurant. The area is a bit unappealing. **www.RoyalStuttgart.de**	3.5 stars

Suggested Lodging in Central Stuttgart

(All selected lodging has 3.5 or better rating)

	Hotel	Address & Details	Rating
8	EmiLu Design Hotel	Nadlerstraße 4 70173 Stuttgart Near the MarktPlatz, a popular spot for major events and open markets. In an active area filled with shops, restaurants, and bars. The Galeria department store is a block away. Several blocks south of Schlossplatz and almost a mile south of the train station. This is a new, modern, and somewhat upscale property providing unique rooms and suites. Amenities include a gourmet breakfast lounge and fitness center. **www.EmiLu-Hotel.com**	4 stars

Airport Hotels: If you wish to stay in the area around the airport, there are several large hotels within walking distance from the terminal. Including:

- Mövenpick Hotels (2 properties here) **www.Movenpick.Accor.com**

- Wyndham Stuttgart Airport: **www.WyndhamHotels.com**

5: Getting Around in Stuttgart

Walking, Light Rail, Bicycles & Hop-On Tours

Stuttgart's center is easy to navigate and find your way around. When staying here, there is little need to have a car in town (unless, of course, you have flown in to pick up your new Porsche or Mercedes). If you plan on getting out of town to visit nearby towns or castles, several rental car companies are available right in town and the local transportation network is superb.

This is an easy town to walk around and explore. The town center is largely flat and traffic along most routes is not bothersome. Several areas are geared more to accommodating pedestrians than vehicles, providing for enjoyable browsing and window shopping. Numerous sidewalk cafes line the more popular streets, which add to the fun of exploring this modern city.

Almost every location in town can be traveled to by walking or taking the local light rail or buses. Bicycle rental is also an option which is growing in popularity, especially for e-bikes.

Most walking distances and times are within a 5-to-20-minute time frame and the walks are generally along pleasant avenues with only moderate traffic.

> **Suggested Area Map App:**
>
> The Stuttgart Map and Walks app is an excellent resource to help you navigate this city.

Example Walking Times in the Center of Stuttgart

The Light Rail (Stadtbahn) System: When it comes to Stuttgart's transportation system for first-time visitors, this is a "Good News/Bad News" situation.

- Good News: This is a very comprehensive system.
- Bad News: The system is so comprehensive that it can be confusing at first and, well, at second and third glance as well.

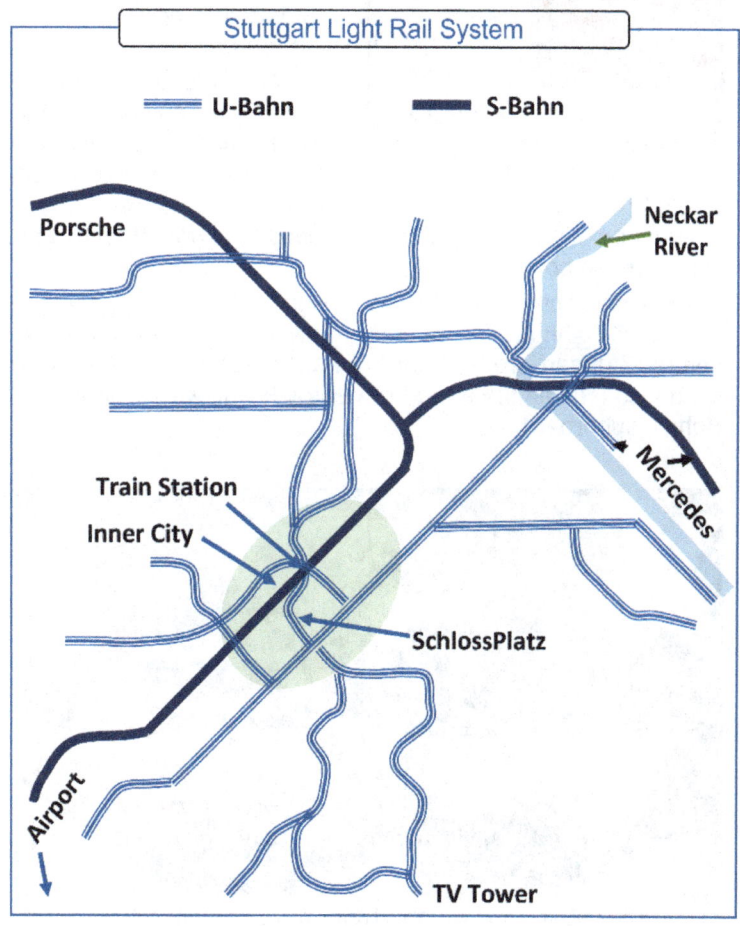

The **VVS Mobil App** provides all info needed to use the Stuttgart light rail system.

The light rail system is a mixture of underground and above ground tracks and stations. The term "subway" is generally not used to describe this system. The more common designators are either the German term "Stadtbahn" or simply call it the tram.

One element that can add to initial confusion is the overlaying of two different networks, the "U-Bahn" and the "S-Bahn." These stations mostly travel to different locations although some stations service both networks.

For simplicity, consider the U-Bahn as the urban network and the S-Bahn as the suburban network. Most stations within central Stuttgart are "U-Bahn" (urban) and trips out of town to such locations as the airport or nearby towns will be on the "S-Bahn" (suburban).

The U-Bahn and S-Bahn Trains have different colors.
U-Bahn trains are Yellow
S-Bahn trains aree Red

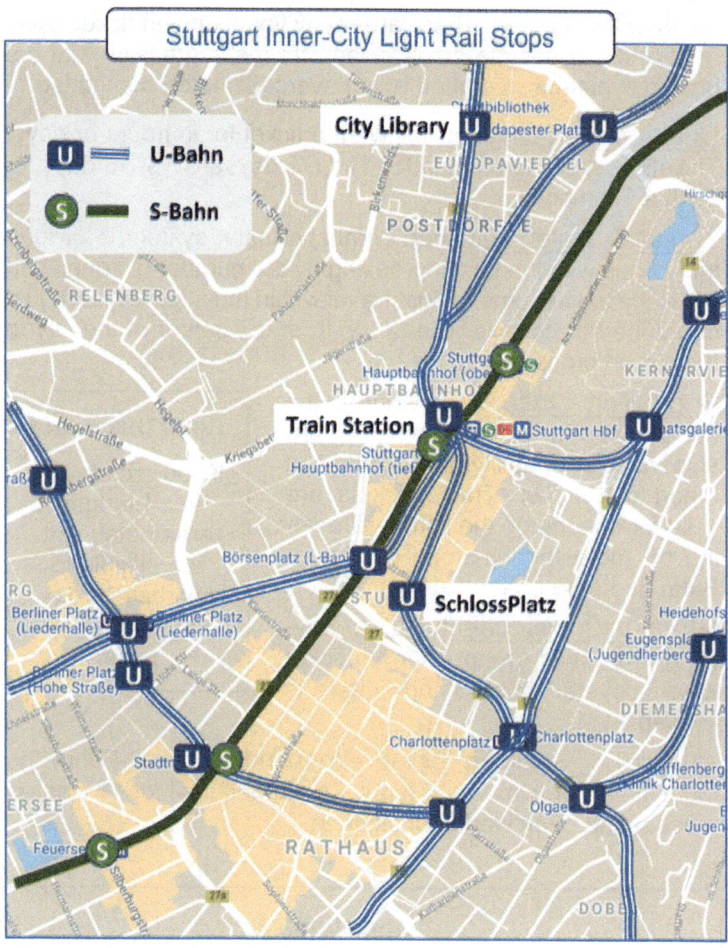

Tram, Subway and Bus Tickets: Tickets work equally well across the network of light rail and buses and may be purchased either online, through the VVS app, numerous vendors in the area, online, or at a light rail station. All rail stations have easy to identify kiosks to purchase tickets. Also, when taking local buses, tickets may be purchased when boarding the bus.

There are, unfortunately, several variables to consider when purchasing tickets which can be daunting for first-time users of this system. There are many variations on ticket types here and it is easy to come away with the impression that the pricing system was crafted by an overcaffeinated committee.[9]

Duration: How long you will want a ticket for in hours or days. Tickets may be purchased for 1-trip, 1-day, 3-days, 10 days, or even a full-month.

Zones Traveled: Stuttgart's transportation system is divided into zones with the cost increasing by the number of zones you will likely travel across. Most travel within the inner city is in just one zone but, for example, a trip from the center of the city to the airport crosses 3 zones.

Short Trip Option: To add to the complexity with distance options, you also have the ability to purchase a "short trip" ticket. These tickets are valid for one trip on the light rail traveling no more then 3-stops on the U-Bahn or 1 stop on the S-Bahn.

Group vs Individual: if you are traveling in a small group, a group ticket which covers up to 5 individuals is available.

Hotel Discounts

If you are staying in a Stuttgart area hotel, you are eligible to purchase a discounted 3-day pass.

1st Class or Standard Ticket: When riding the S-Bahn, the trains have two classes of fares. The added cost for 1st class is modest and often worth considering.

Suggestion:
Consider simply purchasing a day ticket which covers 3-zones for each day you will be using the local network. This is easy to do at any of the ticket kiosks and will cover most travel needs.

---

[9] **Just for some fun**: Okay, if you want to build your stress level a bit, visit the **VVS.de** website and then browse the numerous pages on ticket prices. This is the easiest they could make pricing, really?

Example Light Rail (Tram and Bus) Pricing [10]

Adult Rates – Purchase tickets via a kiosk at any stop
Online rates via the app, advance purchase is slightly less than
the rates depicted here.

Trip Type	1 Trip	1 Day	Other
Short-Haul Trip	€ 1,70	N/A	N/A
1 Zone	€ 2,90	€ 6,20	1–Week 23,9€
3 Zones	€ 4,80	€ 10,40	1-Week 40,4€
Group -3 Zones	N /A	€ 17,10	N / A
Hotel Discount	N/A	N/A	3 -Day € 15,10

Using Light Rail Tickets: Each ticket must be validated upon entering a train or bus. There are brightly colored boxes on the local buses or U-Bahn trains. When taking an S-Bahn trip, these validation boxes are at the ticket dispensing machines and at the entrance to stations.

Light Rail Ticket Validator

This is largely an honor system as you are not forced to validate a ticket before boarding. Failure to have a valid and validated ticket can be costly as fines are charged if you have not properly followed

---

[10] **Trip Pricing Note:** Data Source is **VVS.De** – the Stuttgart area transportation network. prices quotes are samples only as of April-2024, are subject to change and do not represent all available pass options.

procedures. If you are fined, a cash payment is required to be paid at the time of the event.

Hop-On/Hop-Off Buses: An enjoyable way to travel the city and explore the area's attractions is to take one of the available "**Stuttgart City Tour**" Hop-on/Hop-off tours. Taking one of these tours enables you to see multiple sights without having to figure out how to navigate the city and area on your own. They also provide the advantage of a narration about the local area which can be very informative.

In Stuttgart, there are 3 primary route bus options. The primary "Blue and Green Routes" start from the center of town and the "Wine Route," begins at the Mercedes-Benz Museum. Note, the Green and Wine routes are seasonal and not available all year.

Hop On Bus / City Tour Website:

www.Hop-On-Hop-Off-Bus.de/Stuttgart

With each route, you can get off the bus at any stop, visit the local area, then get back on as it suits you. Many, not all, of Stuttgart's attractions may be reached by taking one of the tours.

Stuttgart City Tour "Hop On" Bus Tours
3 Tour Routes to Select From

Blue Route
9 Stops
1 Hr 40
Minutes

Wine Route
7 Stops
35 Minutes

Mercedes

Inner City

Green Route
8 Stops
1 Hour

TV Tower

Neckar River

Frequency Caution: The buses generally run just once per hour at the most, unlike some cities where the hop-on tours run more frequently.

Blue Route: The most popular route and the only one which operates all year. This route departs from central Stuttgart and includes sights in the center of town, some of the wine area, and the Mercedes Museum. The total time is a little over 1 ½ hours. Popular stops include the Wilhelma Botanical Gardens, the Pig Museum, and Rosenstein Castle. This route runs all year and buses depart a minimum of 1 per hour from mid-morning to 4pm.

Green Route: Availability of this route is limited to April to October and does not run every day. Like the Blue Route, it starts at the Tourist Office near the train station and travels through the central part of town. Much of this 1-hour route is into the hilly area south of town and the stops include the popular Television Tower and lookout points. NOTE: there is limited daily frequency of 5 times per day, so you may want to think twice before hopping off as it can be quite a while before the next bus shows up.

Wine Route: This route is a great way to visit several area wineries and the Stuttgart Museum of Viniculture. This is a smaller, open-air bus which departs from the Mercedes Museum. (Connections to the Blue Route may be made here). The route travels through the hilly eastern area of Stuttgart and has 6 stops including several wineries. The route, if taken without getting off, lasts 35 minutes. Availability is limited to April to October and only from Friday to Sunday.

Hop-On Tickets: Tickets may be purchased directly from the driver, the Stuttgart Tourist Office, or from several online sources. Leading sites which provide these passes include and are not limited to:

- Stuttgart-Tourist.de
- GetYourGuide.com
- Viator.com
- Hop-on-hop-off-bus.de

Stuttgart Hop-On Tour Pricing As of April 2024, and subject to change		
Route	**Adult**	**Child**
Green or Blue	€ 20	€ 5
Wine Route	€ 14	€ 5
Combo: Any 2 routes	€ 30	€ 10

Bike Rental in Central Stuttgart: Stuttgart is a great area for bicycling. The city center is generally flat and accommodating to bicyclists. If you wish to get out into the nearby hills with the many trails, parks and vineyards, it is easy to do so.

There are many firms which rent bicycles here and some firms provide bicycle tours and excursions into the Black Forest.

If your goal is to explore Stuttgart and its neighborhoods, the bike share service Regiorad is highly recommended. This is a city-wide service where you simply need to go to a nearby rental kiosk, select a bike, then return it to any station of your choosing, (which has available slots) when done.

Using this system requires downloading their app from your preferred app store, the "Regio-Rad Stuttgart" app. Then, set up your account and put in credit card info. Once this is done, the firm has made it easy to locate and rent available bikes.

The RegioRad App is needed to use the bike sharing system in Stuttgart.

Cost varies by how long you use a bike and is metered by the minute. The maximum cost for a regular bike is € 9 per day or €16 per day for an electric bike.

The app provides a detailed map on available stations and bikes.

www.RegioRadStuttgart.de

6: Inner City Points of Interest

Stuttgart's main attractions are spread out with several in the inner city and many of the more popular destinations on the city's outskirts.

This chapter outlines the more popular attractions and sights right in town, the "Inner City." The next chapter details the most popular sights on the edge of town. Each of this second group will require either driving to them, taking local transportation, or using one of the Hop-On tours.

This inner city has an interesting mix of attractions which range from the normal and expected art and history museums to the unusual such as the City Library.

For nature and food lovers, Stuttgart offers large parks to stroll through and numerous restaurants with local cuisine. About half of the popular sights in and around Stuttgart are in the Inner City. Twelve of them are outlined here.

Each of the sites shown in the following map below are detailed in the following section on Inner-City attractions. Locations are listed simply in a north-to-south order.

Recommended App for Stuttgart Attractions: Download the "Stuttgart City Guide" app for details on the city's attractions, and interactive maps. There is a modest fee for this app.

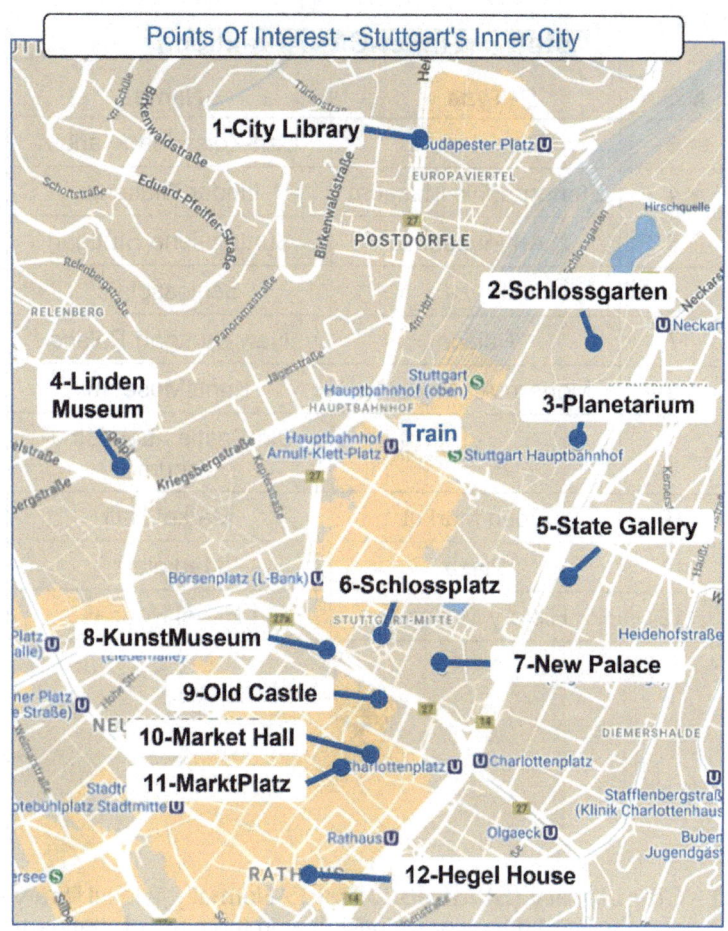

Points Of Interest - Stuttgart's Inner City

1-City Library
2-Schlossgarten
3-Planetarium
4-Linden Museum
5-State Gallery
6-Schlossplatz
7-New Palace
8-KunstMuseum
9-Old Castle
10-Market Hall
11-MarktPlatz
12-Hegel House

Stuttgart Inner-City Attractions		
Map #	Type	Name
1	Library	Stadtbibliothek
2	Park	Mittlerer Schlossgarten

Stuttgart Inner-City Attractions		
Map #	Type	Name
3	Planetarium	Carl-Zeiss Planetarium
4	Ethnographic Museum	Linden Museum
5	Art Museum	Stattsgalerie Stuttgart
6	Plaza	Schlossplatz
7	Palace	New Stuttgart Palace
8	Modern Art Museum	KuntsMuseum
9	History Museum	Old Castle / Landsmu-seum
10	Open Market	Market Hall
11	Plaza	Markplatz
12	History Museum	Hegel House

1 - City Library (Stadtbibliothek): Normally, a local library is not on a list of attractions to visit but, in the case of Stuttgart, the City Library (Stadtbibliothek Stuttgart) is worth visiting as the modern design is an architectural delight.

This 8-floor building is a spacious and airy facility with collections in several media, not just books. It opened in 2011 and has become one of Stuttgart's most photographed places. After strolling through the collections, consider relaxing in the brightly lit café on the upper floor.

Stuttgart City Library / Stadtbibliothek

- **Entrance Fee**: There is no charge to enter.

- **Address**: Mailänder Platz 1, 70173 Stuttgart

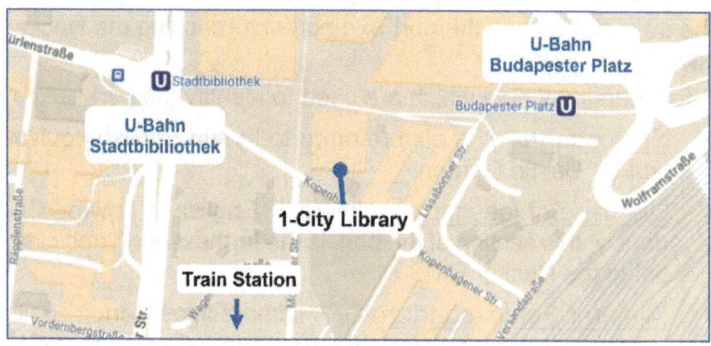

- **Light Rail Stop**: Two U-Bahn stations are close to the library. The shortest walk is from the Stadtbibliothek station which is serviced by lines U-5, U-6, U-7 and U-15. It is less than a five-minute walk from this station to the library.

- Facilities: Restrooms. There is a café on the top floor. Audio guides with headphones are available at the entrance.

- Hours: Open most days from 9 AM to 9 PM. Closed on Sunday.

- Nearby: This area is a modern office park with several restaurants and shops close by.

- Website: **www.Stadtbibliothek-Stuttgart.de**

2 - Schlossgarten / Schloßgarten: The naming gets to be a bit confusing as this long park has multiple sections with differing names along the way. Schlossgarten is part of a connected group of parks in Stuttgart's center. It stretches for roughly 1 ½ miles (Over 2 kilometers) with its southern end near the train station and the northern portions reaching the Neckar River.

A few names of note which are used to identify the park:

- Schlossgarten: Is also referred to by the English equivalent of "Castle Garden"

- Unterer Schlossgarten: Unterer in English is "Lower." Curiously, this section of the park is the furthest north and closest to the Neckar River.

- Mittlerer Schlossgarten: Or "Middle Schlossgarten". This is the section which stretches from the train station northward.

- Oberer Schlossgarten: "Upper Schlossgarten" is the smallest of the three sections and stretches southward from the train station for roughly three blocks.

In size, the park covers nearly 160 acres (64 hectares). Attractions in the park are numerous including:

- Several ponds and small lakes.
- Children's play area
- Planetarium
- Beer garden
- Bike paths
- Thermal baths
- Sports fields
- Numerous statues

Schlossgarten Layout

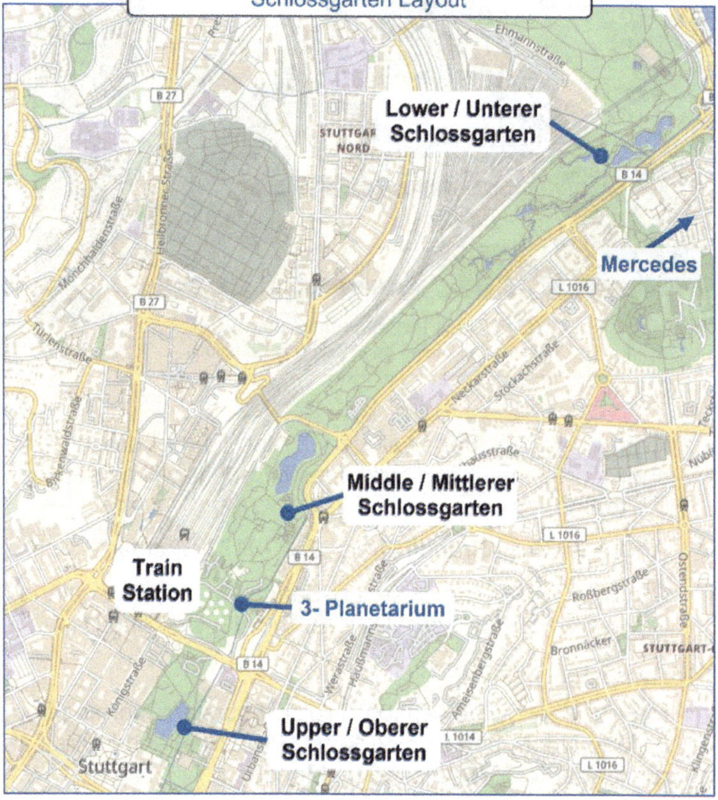

Lower / Unterer Schlossgarten

Mercedes

Middle / Mittlerer Schlossgarten

Train Station

3- Planetarium

Upper / Oberer Schlossgarten

3 - Planetarium / Carl Zeiss Planetarium: Sitting only two blocks from the train station is a recently updated and expanded planetarium which is a fun site to view space exhibits. Stuttgart has had a planetarium in this location since 1977. It was completely remodeled in 2016 and now offers a multi-faced space program with such programs as "The Planets" and "Time Travel". For fun, even concerts are held "under the stars" here. All programs are available in English via headsets.

Carl Ziess Planetarium Stuttgart
Photo source: Stefan Xp - Wikimedia Commons

- Entrance Fee: Fees will vary by the time of day and the shows presented. Typically, fees for adults will be between 5 € to 8 €.

- Address: Willy-Brandt-Straße 25, 70173 Stuttgart

- Subway Stop: The closest U-Bahn stop is "Staatsgalerie." Several lines stop here: U1, U2, U4, U9, U11 and U14.

- Facilities: Restrooms.

- Hours: Vary by the season. Typical hours are morning from 8AM to Noon, and from 2PM to 4PM. Weekend hours can run longer to 7 PM Closed on Monday.

- Website: **www.Planetarium-Stuttgart.de**

4 - Linden-Museum Stuttgart: The museum defines itself as "A world trip under one roof." Collections here include displays from every continent and sub-continent. The museum opened in 1911 to inform visitors about the numerous cultures outside of Europe. It is deemed to be an "ethnology" museum which is the study of differing characteristics of various cultures and cross-cultural interactions.

The Linden Museum - a "Museum of Culture."
Photo source: Julian Herzog - Wikimedia Commons

Over 160,000 items are housed here. This museum can be reached by a 15-minute walk from the center of town along a pleasant path which takes you through the university area.

- Entrance Fee: There is a €4 fee to visit the permanent exhibits. Special exhibits are an added fee and may vary. Free if you have a StuttCard. (See Preface for StuttCard details.)

- Address: Hegelplatz 1, 70174 Stuttgart

- Tram & Bus Stops: There are no light rail or subway stops adjacent to the museum. Two stations, each served by the U4 line, are about a 7-minute walk. These are the Berliner-Platz and Rosenberg-Seidenstraße stations. Bus lines 40 & 42 s stop directly in front of the museum.

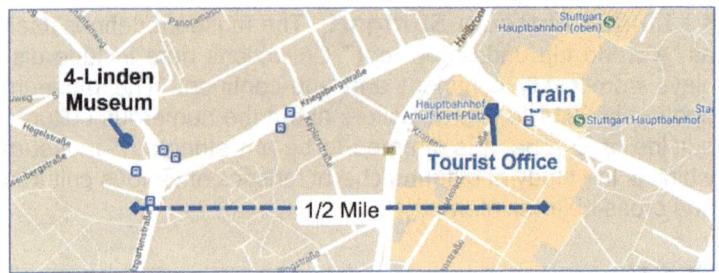

- **Hop-On Bus Stop:** Both the Blue and Green routes stop near the Linden Museum.

- **Facilities:** A coffee shop is on site along with restrooms and a small gift shop.

- **Hours:** Open Tuesday to Saturday from 10 AM to 5 PM. Sunday from 10 AM to 6 PM. Closed on Monday.

- **Nearby:** The university is across the street but there is little in the way of shopping or restaurants in the immediate vicinity of this museum.

- **Website: www.LindenMuseum.de**

5 - State Gallery (Staatsgalerie Stuttgart): A popular, large, and expansive art gallery which displays many major works across three interconnected buildings. The works span over 8 centuries from renaissance to impressionism and modern. Masterpieces such as those from Picasso, Klee, Matisse, and many others may be found here.

The two largest structures in this complex are: Old/Alte Staatsgalerie: This large structure is also the site of the Royal Art School. Collections are focused on art from the 14th century to early twentieth century including the Romanticism and

Impressionism periods. And New/Neue Staatsgalerie: the focus of this recently built facility is on modern art.

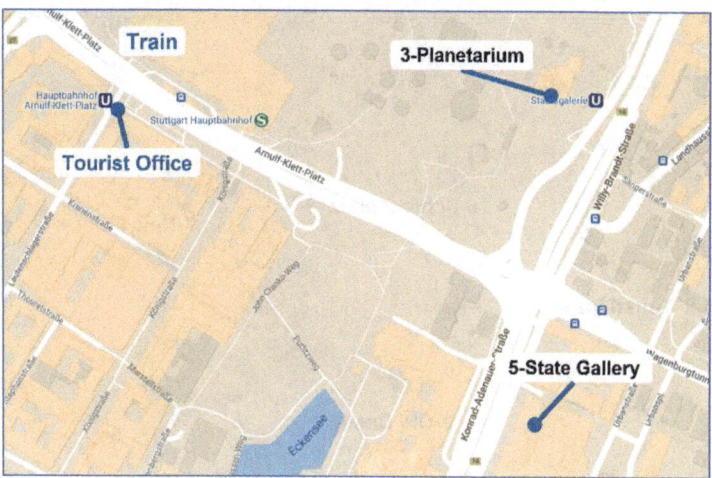

- Address: Konrad-Adenauer-Str.30, 70173 Stuttgart.

- Tram & Bus Stops: Stattsgalerie station. This station is a 5-minute walk from the museum. Lines: U1, U2, U4, U9 and U14 stop here.

- Facilities: Restaurant, café, gift shop and toilets. Audio guides with headphones are available at the entrance.

- Hours: Open Tuesday to Saturday from 10 AM to 5 PM. Thursday open until 8 PM. Closed on Monday.

- Nearby: The museum sits along a busy road and there are very few shops and restaurants in the immediate vicinity.

- Website: **www.LindenMuseum.de**

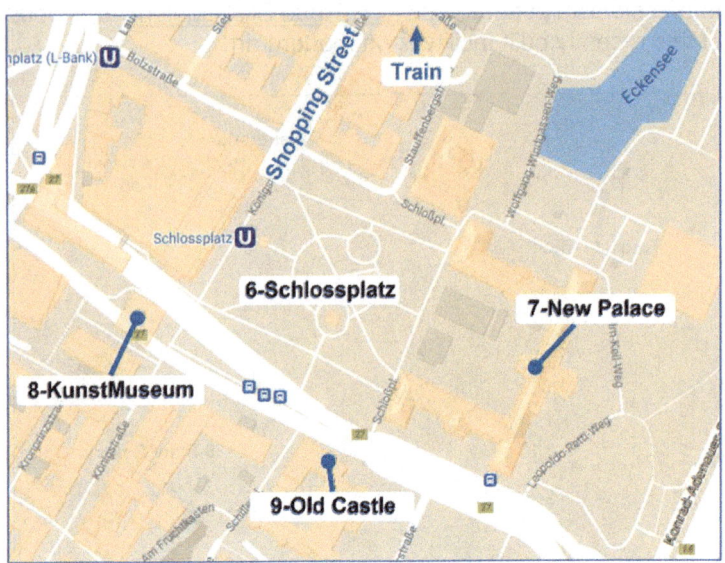

6 & 7- Schloss Platz & New Palace: [11] The heart of

Stuttgart's Inner City is the large <u>Schlossplatz (Palace Square)</u> and adjoining New Palace. The plaza is the hub of this city, and it makes a great starting point for explorations. While Marktplatz may be the location for open markets, Schlossplatz is the location where many concerts are held. With the several pools and fountains, it also is a great place to sit and relax on a sunny day.

The plaza was once a military parade ground, which made for proud processions with the palace as a backdrop. Along one side of the plaza is the popular shopping street<u>, Königstraße</u>. In the immediate vicinity is the Old Castle and the modern art museum.

---

[11] **New Palace / New Castle:** The two names are in common use, with New Stuttgart Palace the more formal. Either name will suffice when referring to this large complex.

Schlossplatz & New Palace (Neues Schloss)
(Schlossplatz is in the foreground with New Palace behind)

The New Palace, (Neues Schloss) is an active center of government for the Baden-Württenberg state. Due to this, the ability to go into the palace and explore is limited. The palace currently holds the Ministries of Finance, Economics, Labor, and Housing. This palace was constructed for the dukes and counts of Württemberg and was constructed over a 60- year span in the last half of the 18th century. Prior to becoming a set of government offices, the palace had been a residence of area (Württemburg) dukes.

The lower level of one wing houses the State Museum, so this part is open to the public.

- Tram & Bus Stops: Multiple U-Bahn lines stop here at the Schlossplatz station.

- Hop-On Bus: Both the Green and Blue Hop-On routes stop here.

- Facilities: Public toilets are next to the plaza.

- Hours: The plaza is open to the public at all hours except for when special events such as concerts are occurring.

- <u>Nearby:</u> Numerous shops and restaurants are in the immediate vicinity in addition to the Old Palace and the Kunst Museum, a modern art museum. In addition, the primary pedestrian shopping street, Königstraße.is here.

- <u>Palace Website</u>: **www.Neues-Schloss-Stuttgart.de**

8 - Museum of Modern Art (Kunstmuseum-Stuttgart):
Opened in 2005, this intriguing museum, built in a contemporary cubic style, includes an array of modern and contemporary pieces. The building has the appearance of a glass cube. At night, when it is lit, people on the outside can see into the interior and its limestone walls. The museum is located on the popular and primary shopping street, the "Königstrasse.

The Modern Art Museum / Kunstmuseum
Adjacent to the Schlossplatz
Photo source: Julian Herzog - Wikimedia Commons

Inside, there are three floors of exhibits above ground and substantial exhibit space below street level. There is nearly 54,000 square feet (5,000 sq meters) of exhibit space to browse.

- Address: Kleiner Schloßplatz 1, 70173 Stuttgart.

- Tram Stop: The museum is immediately next to the Schlossplatz station which is serviced by several U-Bahn lines.

- Hop-On Bus: Both the Blue and Green Hop-On routes visit the Schlossplatz which is adjacent to this museum.

- Facilities: Toilets and a gift shop. There is a restaurant on the upper level with a 360 view of the inner city.

- Hours: Tuesday to Sunday 10 AM to 5 PM. Friday, open until 8 PM and closed on Monday.

- Nearby: The museum is on the main shopping street and next to the Schlossplatz. This locale is a focal point in Stuttgart for restaurants and shops.

- Website: **www.Kuntsmuseum-Stuttgart.de**

9 - State History Museum & Old Castle (Landesmuseum Württemberg & Altes Schloss): A visit to the Old Castle, Altes Schloss, and visiting the State History Museum (Wurttemberg State Museum), is essentially one in the same as the museum takes up much of the interior of the expansive complex.

The Old Castle grew out of an old fortress. In the 16th century, this castle and court hall were expanded and remodeled to become a prominent renaissance palace. A unique feature of the 4-story structure is a passage that was built so the top floor, where the Knight's Hall is, could be reached by horse.

Courtyard in Stuttgart's "Old Castle" (Altes Schloss)

When the New Palace was built in the 18th century, this castle was relegated to house lesser authorities. The building has undergone several bad periods in recent times. In the 1930's much of it was destroyed in a fire and in WWII bombs heavily damaged the building again. Starting in the 1960s the castle underwent a major rebuild and is one of the few major structures in Stuttgart which was built to match its former design.

Today, the Old Castle contains the Wurttemberg State Museum (History Museum) which is the most prominent attraction housed here. This is the primary and most comprehensive history museum in the area dedicated to the German region of Baden-Württemberg. The expansive collections are housed in several buildings, but the primary collection is in the Old Castle near the center of the city.

Items on display include local archeology, musical instruments, historical furniture, fashion, artifacts from the Middle Ages and Celtic periods, and folklore.

- Address: Schillerplatz 6, 70173 Stuttgart

- Tram Stop: The museum is immediately next to the Schlossplatz station which is serviced by several U-Bahn lines. OR, a good alternative is the Charlottenplatz station which is just a 3 minute walk from the museum. It is also serviced by several U-Bahn lines.

- Hop-On Bus: Both the Blue and Green Hop-On routes visit the Schlossplatz which is adjacent to this museum.

- Facilities: Toilets and a gift shop. There is also a fairly large coffee shop on site.

- Hours: Tuesday to Sunday 10 AM to 5 PM. Closed on Monday.

- Nearby: Across from the popular Schlossplatz and New Palace. Also, very close to the large Market Hall which is just one block south.

- Website: www.LandesMuseum-Stuttgart.de

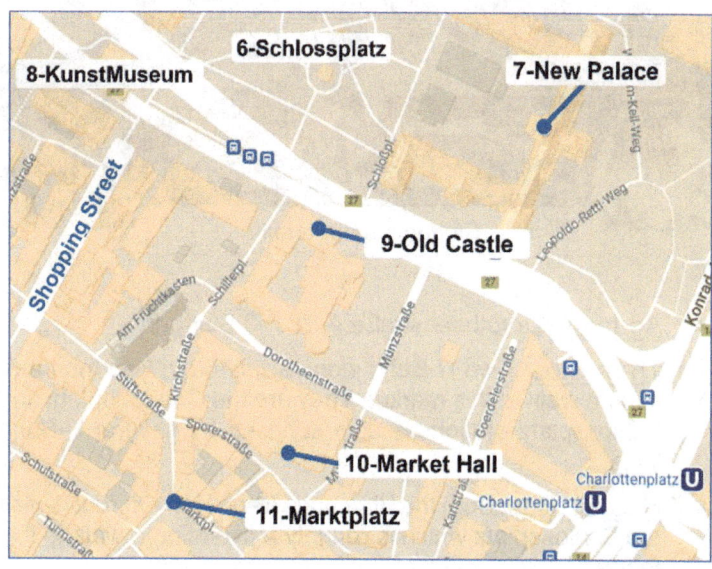

10 - Market Hall (Stuttgarter Markthalle): A short distance south of Schlossplatz is a large covered market. This popular market has been in existence for more than one hundred years and is an active center for shopping. With dozens of booths on two floors, there is a broad array of gourmet foods and gift items. There are nearly 54,000 square feet (5,000 sq meters) of space in this large market with dozens of permanent stalls.

The market hall is in an Art Nouveau building with a glass roof, giving it an open and sophisticated feel.

Stuttgart Market Hall

- Address: Dorotheenstraße 4, 70173 Stuttgart

- Tram Stop: Two U-Bahn stops are nearby, less than a 5-minute walk to this market. They are the Charlotteplatz and Schlossplatz stations.is also serviced by several U-Bahn lines.

- Hop-On Bus: Both the Blue and Green Hop-On routes visit the Schlossplatz which is roughly a five-minute walk to this market.

- <u>Facilities</u>: Several small restaurants and seating areas are in this building including one which focuses on Swabian cuisine. (This is the regional cuisine. There is also an Italian restaurant and a popular Tapas bar.

- <u>Hours</u>: Normal hours: Monday to Friday from 7:30 AM to 6:30 PM. Saturdays are from 7 AM to 5 PM. Closed Sunday.

- <u>Nearby</u>: This shopping/market hall is in the center of much of the Inner City's shopping and dining area. A block south is the Marktplatz, which is the focal point for Stuttgart's Christmas market.

- <u>Website</u>: **www.Markthalle-Stuttgart.de**

11 - Market Square (Marktplatz): This is an open square a short distance from the much larger Schlossplatz. During WWII, this area was heavily bombed, so most of what is here is

Market Square / Marktplatz
A popular site for open markets, especially on weekends.
Photo source: Joma2411 - Wikipedia

relatively new. The Stuttgart City Hall lines one side of the plaza. A complete facelift and redesign was given to this square in 2020.

A leading reason to come here is to explore the open market which is held every Tuesday, Thursday, and Saturday morning. Other notable events are also held here including the Stuttgart Christmas Market, the Festival of Cultures each summer, and the Stuttgart wine festival each August.

- Address: Marktplatz, 70173 Stuttgart

- Tram Stop: The Rathaus U-Bahn station is a three-minute walk away. This station is served by U1, U2, U4,U9, U11 and U14 lines.

- Hop-On Bus: Both the Blue and Green Hop-On routes visit the Schlossplatz which is roughly a five-minute walk to this plaza.

- Facilities: This plaza is surrounded by shops and restaurants. Major stores such as Breitling clothing are here. The Stuttgart Town Hall lines one side of the square

- Hours: The plaza is always open. Open markets are held every Tuesday, Thursday and Saturday.

- Nearby: The large Market Hall is just one block north from this plaza.

12 – Hegel House (Hegelhaus): This is a small museum south of Marktplatz which is dedicated to the German philosopher, George Wilhelm Hegel and it is where was born and raised. Exhibits are on his philosophical works, life story. Visit only if you have an interest in this philosopher or German philosophy as it is small with only a few notable exhibits.

Hegel House Museum
Photo source: Wikimedia Commons

- Address: Eberhardstrae 53, 70173 Stuttgart
- Tram Stop: The Rathaus U-Bahn station is less than a five-minute walk.
- Hours: Normal hours are Monday to Saturday from 10 AM to 6 PM with a one-hour closure for lunch. Closed on Sunday.
- Website: **www.Hegel-Haus.de**

7: Attractions on the Edge of Town

Several of Stuttgart's most popular attractions are on the edge of the city and most are not within walking distance. The good news is that all of these sites are easy to reach by train or hop-on bus. Taxis are generally not needed.

Popular Attractions on the Edge of Town

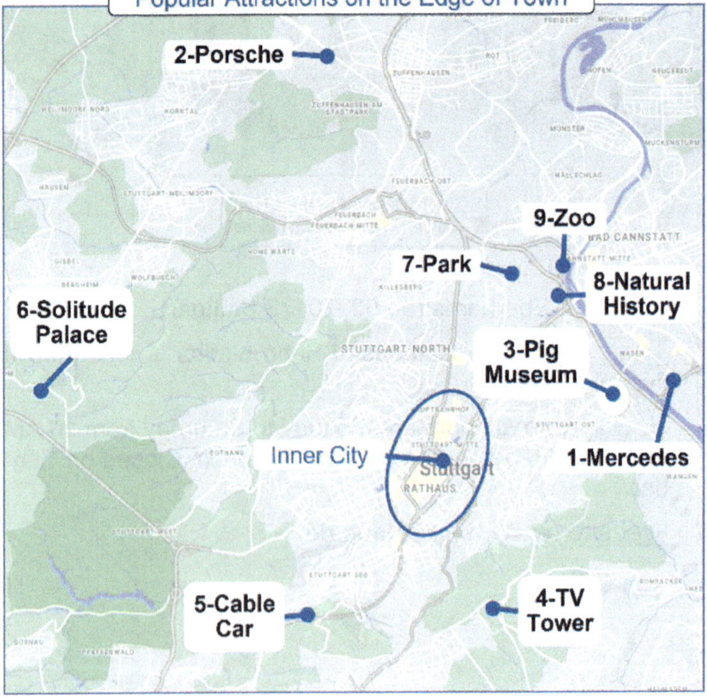

2-Porsche
9-Zoo
BAD CANNSTATT
7-Park
8-Natural History
6-Solitude Palace
STUTTGART-NORTH
3-Pig Museum
Inner City
Stuttgart
RATHAUS
1-Mercedes
5-Cable Car
4-TV Tower

Attractions on the Edge of Stuttgart		
Map #	Type	Name
1	Automotive Museum	Mercedes Benz Museum
2	Automotive Museum	Porsche Museum
3	Peculiar Museum	Pig Museum
4	Tower with Views	Fernsehturm
5	Cable Car	Standseilbahn
6	Palace	Solitude Palace
7	Park	Rosenstein Park
8	Museum	Natural History Museum
9	Zoo	Wilhelma Zoo

1 - Mercedes-Benz Museum: For any car or history lover, a visit to the Mercedes-Benz Museum is a must. Covering nine floors with more than 1,500 exhibits including over 150 historical vehicles, there is enough to delight any visitor.

Plan on a minimum of a half-day to visit here and, if your schedule allows, perhaps even a full day. This museum sits across the Neckar River from Stuttgart's Inner City and generally requires that you travel to it via auto or local transportation.

The exhibits cover automotive history dating back to 1887. In addition to historical exhibits, the museum looks to the future with prototypes and upcoming developments.

On the upper floor of the museum is "Bertha's Restaurant," a full-service restaurant and café with refined and innovative dishes. After your visit to this museum, if you are looking for a change of pace, the hillsides to the west have numerous vine-yards and wine tasting opportunities.

One of many impressive exhibits at the
Mercedes-Benz Museum
Photo source: Mercedes-Benz Museum

- **Entry Fee:** Adult day tickets are € 16. Children 's rate is €8. (As of April-2024 and subject to change)

- **Address:** Mercedesstraße 100, 70372 Stuttgart

- **Tram Stop:** Both the S-Bahn and U-Bahn train lines stop near here. The S-Bahn is closer. Take the S-Bahn to

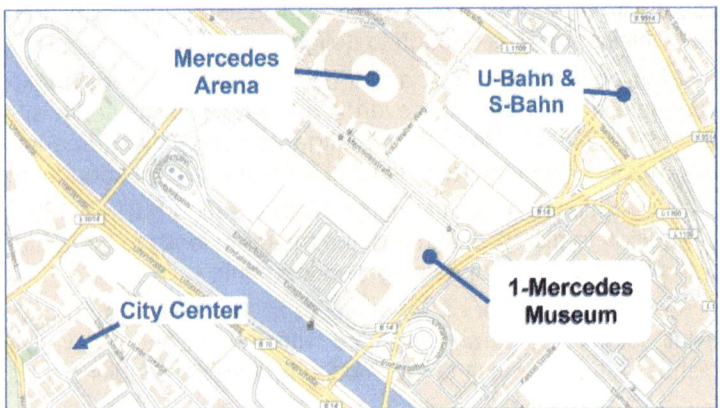

Neckerpark and then walk for roughly 10 minutes. OR, take the bus, which stops directly in front of the museum. Get off at the Mercedes-Benz Welt stop.

- <u>Hop-On Bus:</u> The Blue and Wine routes stop here. This is the point where the Wine route starts and finishes.

- <u>Facilities</u>: Full-service restaurant, gift shop and toilets. Disabled access is provided, and a separate children's area is available. Guided tours are available as well.

- <u>Hours</u>: Normal hours: Tuesday to Sunday from 9 AM to 6 PM. Closed on Monday.

- <u>Website</u>: **museum.mercedes-benz-classic.com**

2 - Porsche Museum: Stuttgart is fortunate to have two world-class automotive museums. Located north of town is the expansive Porsche complex including the ultra-modern Porsche Museum.

This museum is on the northern edge of town and is easy to reach by train and the S-Bahn stops immediately next to the

museum. The focus of the museum is naturally sports cars and their manufacture.

Photo source: Nathanael Burton - Wikimedia Commons

Over 100 cars ranging from historic to futuristic are on display. Plan on spending several hours when coming here.

For children, there is the "Porsche 4Kids" with interactive exhibits designed specifically for children of differing age groups to gain educational experiences.

- Entry Fee: Adults are € 12. Children 's rate is € 6. Porsche club members receive a discounted rate.

- Address: Porscheplatz 1, 70435 Stuttgart

- Tram Stop: Take the S-Bahn (Not the more local U-Bahn) train to the Neuwirtshaus / Porscheplatz station. Lines S6 and S60

- Hop-On Bus: No. None of the Hop-On routes stop here.

- Facilities: Full-service restaurant, gift shop and toilets. Disabled access is provided, and a separate children's area is available. Guided tours are available as well.

- Hours: Normal hours: Tuesday to Sunday from 9 AM to 6 PM. Closed on Monday.

- Website: **www.Porsche.com/Museum**

3 - The Pig Museum (Schweine-Museum): For a bit of whimsy, and a complete change of pace after visiting the Mercedes Museum, just across the river is the Pig Museum.

The Pig Museum / Schweine-Museum

Surprisingly, this quirky facility is one of Stuttgart's most popular sights. The museum and adjoining restaurant are in a former slaughterhouse. Now, there are displays focused on pig (porcine) culture, wild pig hunting, different pig breeds, and pig gastronomy.

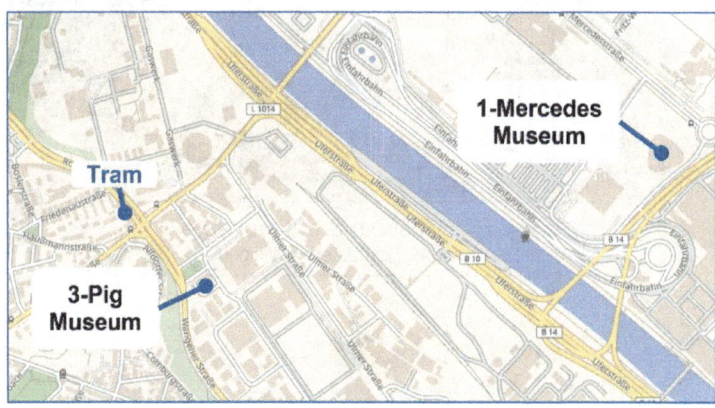

This is the world's largest museum devoted to pigs and pig-related history. There are over two dozen rooms here, each with their own theme such as colorful pigs, or pig versatility, and even pig sex.

- Entry Fee: Adults are € 5,90. Children 's rate is € 3. No fee if you have Stuttcard, the local travel discount card.

- Address: Schlachthofstraße 2A, 70188 Stuttgart

- Tram Stop: Take the U-Bahn, line U9 to Schlachtof station. This is less than a five-minute walk to the museum.

- Hop-On Bus: The Blue route stops here.

- Facilities: Full-service restaurant, gift shop, and toilets. Not surprisingly, the restaurant's menu focuses on pork delights and German beer. Disabled access. Tours are available.

- Hours: Normal hours: Tuesday to Sunday from 10 AM to 5 PM. Closed on Monday.

- Website: **www.SchweineMuseum.de**

The Pig Museum & outdoor cafe
Photo source: Extrastern - Wikipedia

4 - Stuttgart TV Tower (Fernsehturm Stuttgart): One of the world's first television towers which not only functions as a transmission tower but houses an observation tower and café. Coming here is a great way to get a view of the entire area as the tower stands over 700 feet tall (217 meters). From the observation deck you can view all of the Neckar Valley which includes Stuttgart, much of the neighboring wine country, and as far as the Black Forest.

This structure, which opened in 1956, has been the prototype for many similar towers in cities around the globe. Now, it is one of Stuttgart's most prominent landmarks. There is an elevator which takes visitors up to the restaurant and observation deck. Tickets are available at the gift shop in the lower level.

The Stuttgart TV Tower
Go to the top and have a meal or just enjoy incredible views.
Photo source: Taxiarchos228 - Wikimedia Commons

- Address: Fernsehturn, Jahnstraße 120, 70597

- Tram Stop: Ruhbank-Fernsehturm station. Lines U7 and U8. It is a 6-minute walk along a pleasant, wooded path to the tower from the station.

- Hop-On Bus: Yes. Take the Green Route. Note, this route is seasonal.

- Facilities: Toilets. Restaurant and bar at observation level. Gift shop. Elevator to top.

- Hours: 10 AM to 10 PM. The café closes at 6 PM on Sunday.

- Nearby: There is little else within walking distance to visit.

- Website: **www.Fernsehturm-Stuttgart.de**

> **Dinner With a View.**
>
> Come here in the evening for dinner and enjoy stunning views of Stuttgart.

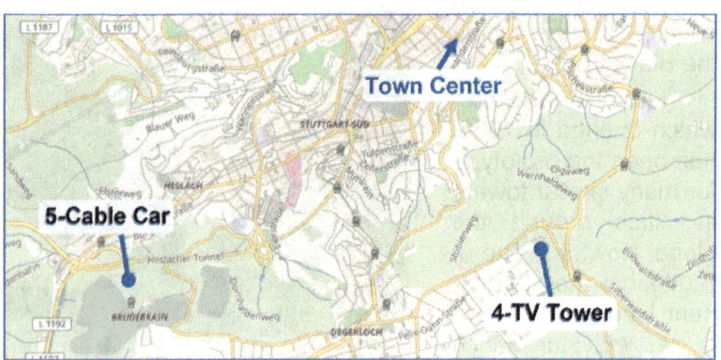

5 - Cable Car/Funicular (Standseilbahn): Slightly southwest from Stuttgart's inner city is an enjoyable cable car (funicular) ride which has been in operation for over 90 years. This was Germany's first cable car of this type. The small train consists of two cars which are made of teak.

This is a laidback adventure which takes riders on a 3-minute journey up almost 300 feet to a large park and cemetery. For individuals interested in rail history, this is an attraction worth checking out. It also provides a nice respite from the busy city below as the park area at the top is large with many trails to explore.

Stuttgart Cable Car / Standseilbahn

Caution: The neighborhood adjacent to the lower-level station is a bit off-putting. So, just focus on a great ride up the hill to the park above and give minimal time to the area at the base.

- Address: Südheimer Platz, 70199 Stuttgart

- Tram Stop: U-Bahn, Südheimer Platz. Lines U1, U9 and U34. The train stop is a 2-minute walk to the cable car.

- Hop-On Bus: The Green Route stops here. Note, this route is seasonal.

- Facilities: Minimal. Toilets and a seasonal snack bar may be found at the top level.

- Nearby: Once you are at the top, there is little in the way of shops and restaurants. There is a snack bar but it is only open during high season. (Summer).

6 - Solitude Palace (Schloss Solitude): Solitude Palace's name is a direct reflection of the intended feel of this Baroque structure. The name specifically implies that this palace stands alone and is not a central part of the active royal court life. This is one of several palaces and country estates built by the Württembergs in the area.

Solitude Palace / Schloss Solitude
Photo source: B. Baendle - Wikimedia Commons

Solitude Palace, a hunting lodge built in the late 18th century, is a place to come to relax and get away from the city in the valley below.

Come here as much for the grounds as the palace. Access to the palace can be limited and often is limited to group tours. If you wish to visit the interior of the palace and its many splendid rooms, it is best to check the website in advance of your visit to see if tours are open for when you plan to visit.

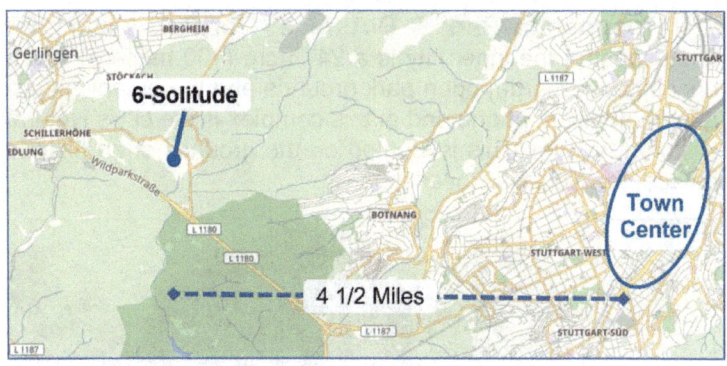

- **Tours:** The standard, "classic" tour is available year-round and is included in the basic entry fee. Other tours are available via the website.

- **Address:** Solitude 1, 70197 Stuttgart

- **Transportation Stop:** No train stations are within an easy walk. The bus (#92) does come directly to the palace. The best way to reach this palace is by private car.

- **Hop-On Bus:** No. This site is not serviced by any of the Hop-On bus routes.

- **Facilities:** Toilets. Guided tours are conducted in German. Limited handicapped access and no elevator to upper floor.

- **Hours:** Castle opening hours vary by the season. During high season from April 1 to Oct 31 hours are from 10 AM to 5 PM Tue to Sunday, closed on Monday. Opening hours for other seasons are similar but with typical closing hours of 4 PM.

- **Website:** **www.Schloss-Solitude.de**

7 – Rosenstein Park & Botanical Garden: A short distance west of the inner city is a 247 acre (100 hectare) which encompasses large, open park grounds and the botanical garden. In addition, at one end of this complex is the city's Natural History Museum. This is located on the grounds of an historic palace, the Schloss Rosenstein.

Formal English Gardens within Rosenstein Park
Photo source: Immanuel Giel - Wikimedia Commons

Impressive Green Spaces.

This park is much more than formal gardens. The open green areas are huge and a great place to relax, run or sun yourself in the summer.

The park has the largest English styled garden in southwest Germany. It was established in int mid-19th century. The park is considered to be part of Stuttgart's "Green U" as it connects with other major parks including Schlossgarten. In addition to the botanical garden, there are expansive green spaces which include small lakes. Underneath the park, and at odds with the peaceful setting, is a busy railroad tunnel, the Rosenstein Tunnel.

Note: this is a large park so knowing how it is laid out can be helpful. The Botanical Gardens is near the southeastern end. The zoo is close to the northwestern end of the park. The Natural History Museum has two buildings, one in the northern sector and one in the park's southern section.

- Entry Fee: There are no fees to enter the park.

- Address: Rosensteinstraße, 70191 Stuttgart

- Tram Stop: Two U-Bahn stations are adjacent to this large park. The Rosensteinpark station is at the park's northern side and the Mineralbäder station is at the southern end which is also close to the natural history museum.

- Hop-On Bus: The Blue Route, which runs all year, stops at the park and neighboring zoo.

- Website: **www.Stuttgart.de** – then search for Rosenstein Park.

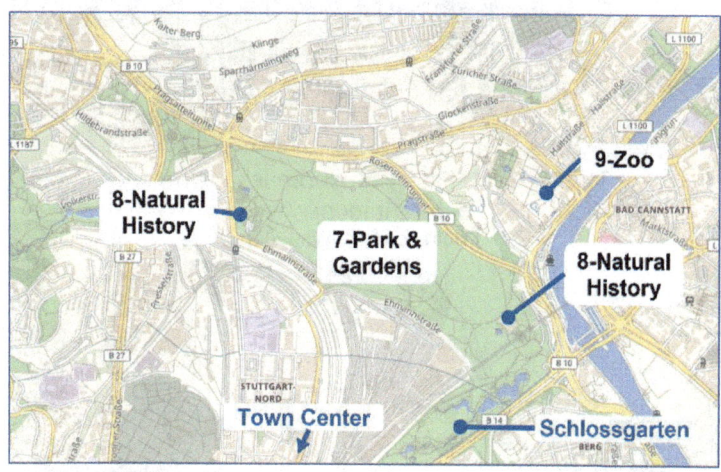

8 – Natural History Museum / Naturkundemuseum: Located in the large Rosenstein Park which is near the Neckar River. This museum complex can be confusing at first as it is divided across two buildings which are almost a mile apart.

- Löwentor Museum – northwestern sector of the park in a modern facility. This building's focus is on paleontology and geology.

- Rosenstein Museum, in the southeastern portion of the park is in a former palace and its focus is on biology and natural history.

The Natural History Museum is in two very different locations.
Photo source: Wikipedia

- <u>Transportation Stop</u>: Two U-Bahn stations should be considered. The Rosensteinpark station is at the park's northern side and close to the Löwentor Museum. The Mineralbäder station is at the southern end, which is near the which is also close to the Rosenstein Museum.

- <u>Hop-On Bus</u>: The Blue Route services both areas of the park where the two museum buildings are located.

- <u>Facilities</u>: Toilets. Gift shops and cafés in each location.

- <u>Hours</u>: Open from 9 AM to 5 PM Tue to Sunday, closed on Monday.

- <u>Website</u>: **www.NaturkundeMuseum-bw.de**

9 – Wilhelma Zoo: East of Stuttgart's inner city and next to the river is Wilhelma Zoo. With over two million visitors each year, it is one of the region's most popular attractions. The zoo covers over 180 acres (74 hectares) and it houses over 11,000 animals representing more than 1,000 species.

- <u>Entry Fee</u>: Rates vary by the season. Normal Adult rate for Spring to Fall is €22 and child rate is € 8,50.

- <u>Hours</u>: Open hours vary by the season. Spring and Summer hours are from 8 AM to 8 PM IF you visit by the main entrance. There is an entrance from the adjacent Rosensteinpark but its hours are shorter.

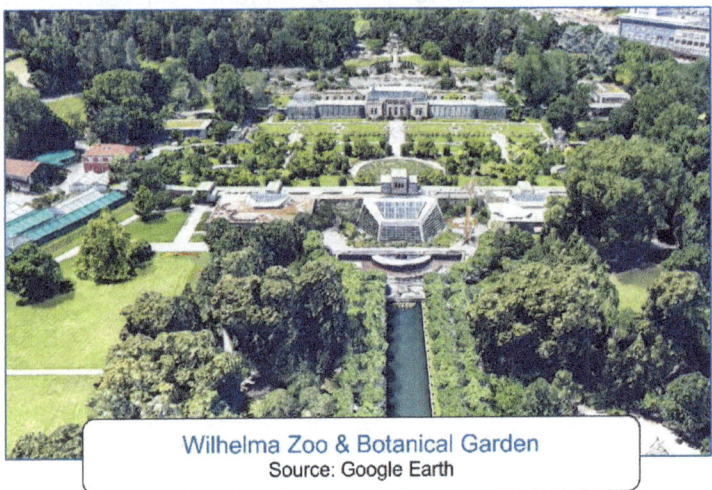

Wilhelma Zoo & Botanical Garden
Source: Google Earth

- **Address**: Wilhelma 13, 70376 Stuttgart

- **Transportation Stop:** The zoo is reachable by U-Bahn, S-Bahn and bus. The best way to travel is by U-Bahn, lines U13, U14 or U16, then get off at the Wilhelma stop which is next to the zoo entrance.

- **Hop-On Bus:** Yes. The Blue Line stops here.

- **Nearby**: This zoo is immediately adjacent to the expansive park grounds of Rosenstein Park. Within this park, is Rosenstein Palace (Schloss Rosenstein) which houses the natural history museum.

- **Facilities:** Toilets. Handicapped access. Café, Gift shops.

- **Website:** **www.Wilhelma.de**

8: Beer Gardens and Swabian Cuisine

This is Germany, so, well, take some time to enjoy some beer/bier. While this is not Bavaria which is so well known for its beerhalls **(Biergartens)** and Oktoberfest, this is a lively area with many great beer halls to sit, relax and enjoy the atmosphere. Stuttgart runs a close second to Munich and Bavaria when it comes to celebrating beer.

The Beer/Bier Garden at Amadeus Bar and Restaurant.
Photo source: Amadeus Bar and Restaurant

You don't need to be here for the annual beer festival (Cannstatt), to enjoy a lively beer garden. Opportunities to kick back in a beer hall or garden abound. In addition to the many

establishments throughout the region, there are several enjoyable destinations right in Stuttgart. In addition to local beer, several of these locales offer the local Swabian cuisine as well.

The following are several suggested spots to enjoy local beer while in Stuttgart and, of course, this is far from the complete list of all enjoyable spots such as these. The biergartens cited here are all in, or very close to, the heart of town, and there are a variety of venues ranging from sitting in a public park, traditional beer halls and even Swabian restaurants.

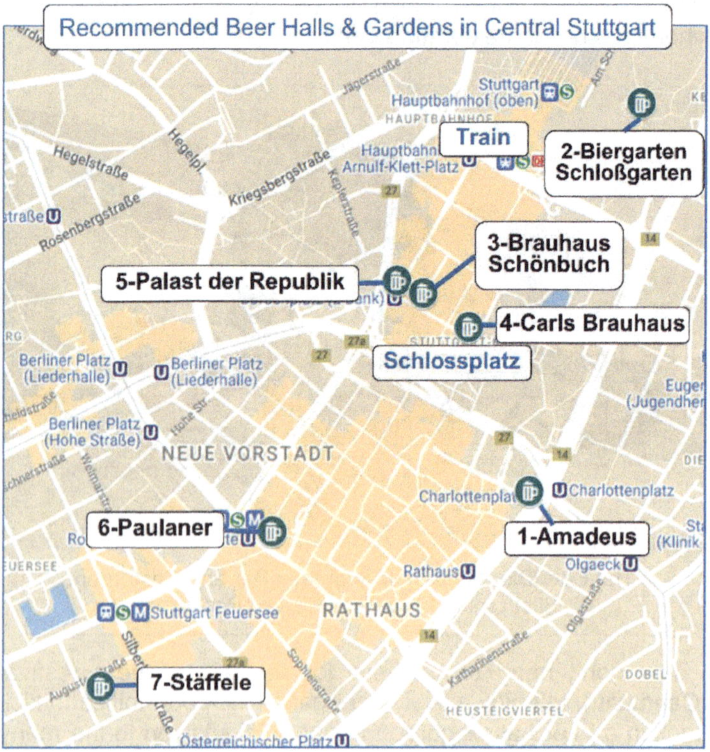

Recommended Beer Halls & Gardens in Central Stuttgart

- Train
- 2-Biergarten Schloßgarten
- 3-Brauhaus Schönbuch
- 5-Palast der Republik
- 4-Carls Brauhaus
- Schlossplatz
- 6-Paulaner
- 1-Amadeus
- 7-Stäffele

Beer Hall & Gardens in Central Stuttgart

Cited in Alphabetic Order

	Beer Hall	Address & Details
1	Amadeus Restaurant and Bar	Charlottenplaz, 17 70173 Stuttgart Beer garden and restaurant serving Swabian cuisine. Indoor and outdoor dining including an enjoyable patio area. A bit up-scale. Located next to Karlsplatz park and close to the Schlossplatz. **www.Amadeus-Stuttgart.de**
2	Biergarten in Schloßgarten **Author Recommendation**	Am Schlossgarten 18 70173 Stuttgart This is the epitome of a German beer garden as it is located in a large park and all seating is outside. This is a very casual, self-service beer stall which often has lively music. Next on the eastern edge of the train station inside the Mittlerer Schlossgarten park. www.**Biergarten-Schlossgarten.de**
3	Brauhaus Schönbuch	Bolzstraße 10 70173 Stuttgart Large restaurant and brewery for the Schönbuch label. A good place to come for a beer or meal. Indoor and patio dining available. In the heart of Stuttgart, near the Schlossplatrz and the major pedestrian shopping street Königstraße. Tucked away off of the main street and a bit hard to find. **www.Brauhaus-Schoenbuch.de**
4	Carls Brauhaus	Stauffenbergstraße 1 70173 Stuttgart

Beer Hall & Gardens in Central Stuttgart

Cited in Alphabetic Order

	Beer Hall	Address & Details
		German restaurant and beer house in the heart of town. Very popular and fills up quickly.(Can be loud – so seek outside seating if available) Located immediately next to the Schlossplatz, giving this a superb location in the heart of town **www.Carls-Brauhaus.de**
5	Palast der Republik	Friedrichstraße 27 70174 Stuttgart This is an interesting experience as it is essentially a large kiosk alongside a small plaza and away from the tourist crowds. The building had previously been a public restroom and it is near a subway stop. Lively and young crowd. Outdoor seating only.
6	Paulaner am alten Postplatz	Calwer Stasse 45 70173 Stuttgart Near the southern sector of central Stuttgart and in a business area. Across the street from the large City Plaza. This large restaurant-brewery (Paulaner label) is very Bavarian in cuisine and feel along with a comprehensive array of Swabian items. Large outdoor dining area and beer garden. www.Paulaner-Stuttgart.de
7	Stuttgarter Stäffele	Buschlestraße 2 a/b 70178 Stuttgart

Beer Hall & Gardens in Central Stuttgart	
Cited in Alphabetic Order	
Beer Hall	**Address & Details**
	The most south-westerly of the establishments cited here. Swabian beer garden and cuisine. Warm, inviting atmosphere and worth the trip from central Stuttgart. **www.Staeffele.de**

Swabian Cuisine: The term "Swabian" is used several times in the descriptions of area beer gardens in this guide. Swabia is the name of the cultural region which defines much of southwest Germany.

Swabian Potato Noodles
One of many regional specialties.

This area has over the years developed its own cuisine which is generally hearty and often rustic. Common Swabian dishes will include such items as local sausages, dumplings, noodles, soups and spätzle.

While in Stuttgart and the area, it is easy to find restaurants which serve these dishes, such as those outlined on the previous pages. Look for such dishes as:

- Noodle and dumpling dishes which may include local meats, spinach and potatoes.

- Spätzel and Knöpfle, a common side dish which may include onions and local cheese.

- Pancakes, also called Flädle, are thin and cooked in oil. Look for Flädle soup where the pancakes are cut into small pieces and placed in a broth.

- Swabian Wursalat: A main dish which includes a mix of area sausages which are sliced and mixed with onions, pickles and chives.

- Swabian Potato Salad, a fairly light salad which will likely include local onions and diced pickles.

- Breads & Treats: Definitely try the area pretzels and bagels. They are often covered in caraway seeds.

Enjoy

9: Castle & Palace Day Trips

Stuttgart and much of the Baden-Württemberg region is rich with castles and palaces. These range from small palaces located in and next to Stuttgart to majestic mountain-top castles a bit further out. There are literally dozens of these historic sites to visit.

This chapter outlines "the best of the best" to explore as day trips. Three castles are detailed which provide a different set of experiences. Visiting all of them is not necessary, but if your schedule allows plan on traveling to at least one as the trip includes travel through beautiful countryside and enables you to explore more than just the Stuttgart metropolitan area.

Traveling to the Castles.

These sites are <u>not</u> easily reached by trains or buses.

Cars are the best way to visit them.

Each of the three castles outlined here are about a one-hour trip each way from central Stuttgart. They also are in remote areas with attractive villages nearby and numerous hiking trails. In addition to the recommended castle outings described here, many other opportunities exist and several of these are outlined at the end of the chapter.

If you are in Stuttgart to pick up a new Porsche or Mercedes-Benz, this is a great opportunity to get out and enjoy the ride. For each location, plan on a minimum of a half-day if you are departing from Stuttgart.

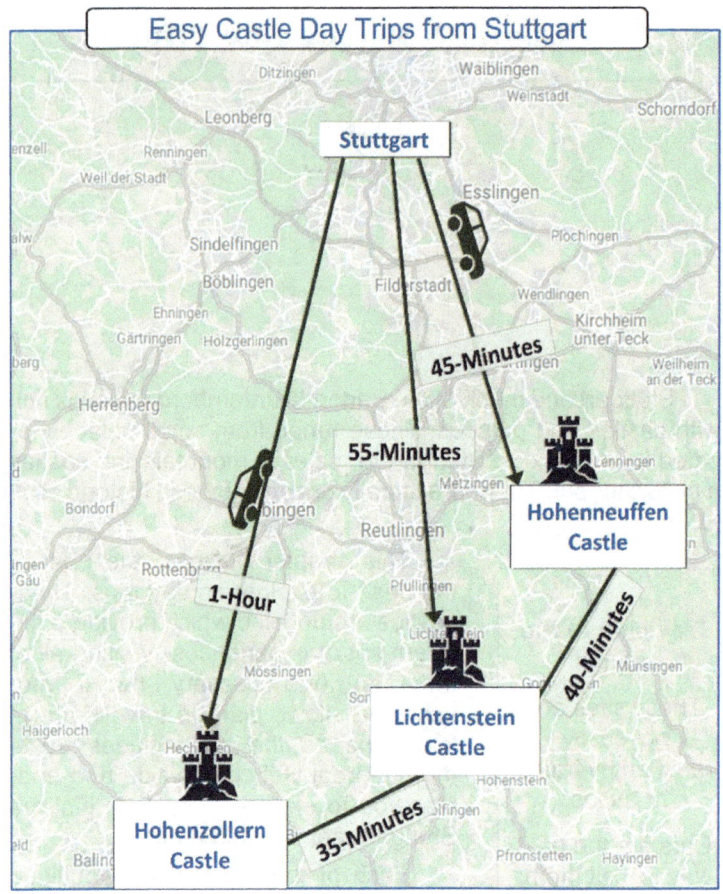

Easy Castle Day Trips from Stuttgart

Stuttgart

45-Minutes

55-Minutes

Hohenneuffen
Castle

1-Hour

40-Minutes

Lichtenstein
Castle

Hohenzollern
Castle

35-Minutes

You can visit more than one Castle in a day.

Combining two of these castles into a one-day visit is easy
to do. Travel between the castles is generally along country roads, much of which is through forested areas.

Hohenzollern-Sigmaringen Castle (Burg Hohenzollern): If you can only visit one castle around Stuttgart, this should be it. This castle, Germany's 2nd largest, has a long history dating back to the 11th century. The structure which currently exists is the third built here. The first was destroyed in the 15th century during a long conflict and the second larger castle later was abandoned. The current, beautiful complex was built as the ancestral seat of the imperial "House of Hohenzollern."

Hohenzollern-Sigmaringen Castle
Perched above the Black Forest

Hohenzollern-Sigmaringen Castle is located on Mt. Hohenzollern and sits over 750 feet above the valley below. This location offers not only great views in every direction, but numerous trails to hike and explore.

The castle today receives over 300,000 visitors annually so it can be crowded in peak season. Much of the palace and grounds are open to view through tours. A tour typically takes one hour and takes you through 20 rooms including the main halls and chapel. Tours are available in German and some in English. Bring a camera as the photo opportunities are numerous.

- Entry Fee: Tickets are slightly less if purchased in advance via the castle website. Full adult price is 25 € and full child rate is 16 €. Discounts are available for: disabled and students. Also, family fares are available.

- Location: A one-hour drive 70 km south from Stuttgart along highway B27. The castle is located near the village of Hechingen.

- Address: Burg Hohenzollern, D-72379 Germany

- How to Get Here: The best way to travel here is by car and it is a pleasant and scenic journey. Trains are available to the nearby village of Landesbahn and a bus goes from there to the castle. However, this train and bus combo can take around two and ½ hours each way. If you are driving, there is a parking area below the castle and a free shuttle from there.

- Facilities: Toilets. Gift shop and a café are on the castle grounds.

- Hours: Hours do vary by season, but typical hours are from 10 AM to 5:30 PM. In the winter, opening hours are 11 AM.

- Tours from Stuttgart: A small number of tours from Stuttgart are available. Most are private tours which can be expensive. Check Viator.com and UniqueGermany.de for current offerings.

- Nearby: The castle sits by itself on a mountaintop and there is little else in the way of shops or restaurants. If you enjoy outdoor activities, there is a network of trails along the hill and just below the castle. Note, if you are driving, the delightful and scenic town of Tübingen is midway between the castle and Stuttgart. (See chapter 10 for more info.)

- Website: **www.Burg-Hohenzollern.com**

Lichtenstein Castle (Schloss Lichtenstein)[12]: A fairy-tale castle perched high above the valley and town of Lichten-stein, accessible by a long and narrow bridge. Built and deco-rated as a hunting lodge in the mid-19th century by Count Wilhelm of Württemberg, the building is charming inside and out.

Lichtenstein Castle
Small but with beautiful views in a dramatic setting.

The castle and adjoining buildings are located in the Swa-bian Alps and provide magnificent views in every direction. Sur-rounding the castle are many trails to explore, a tavern, and even a ropes course.

A visit to the interior of the castle requires joining a tour at the castle (not from Stuttgart). The tours are conducted in Ger-man, but helpful guide info in English will be provided. The tours include several stairways, and no elevators are available. Tours take 30 minutes and cover the main rooms which are exten-sively decorated

---

[12] **Liechtenstein the Country:** It can be confusing, but this castle, near the village of Lichtenstein, is NOT in the country of Liechtenstein. That small country is a 2-hour drive south and has its own castle and a slightly different spelling.

- Entry Fees: There are two fee brackets, one just to visit the grounds and another which includes a guided tour of the interior, plus admission to the courtyard grounds. There is also a small parking fee.
  - Castle Courtyard Only: Adult 4 € / Children 2 €
  - Interior Tour & Grounds: Adult 12 € / Children 6 €
- Location: A 55-minute drive south from Stuttgart along a pleasant mix of highway and back road. The nearest town is Lichtenstein (this is the German town, not the country).
- How to Get Here: The best way to travel is by car. There is paid parking near the castle. Train bus combinations are available and total travel time is roughly 90-minutes each way. Take the train to Reutlingen, then a bus departs regularly to the castle. A parking area is below the castle and a free shuttle from there
- Facilities: Toilets, Castle Courtyard Tavern. Note: Mobility impaired should not attempt to take the castle tour as there are many steps and no elevator.
- Hours: Closed January and February. Hours for other months vary by the season. High season hours are 9AM to 5:30 PM.
- Tours from Stuttgart: No structured group tours are available from Stuttgart.
- Nearby: On the castle grounds, there is a tavern and a ropes course. There are also many trails to explore. The attractive town of Lichtenstein sits in the valley below and the Olgahöhle caverns are nearby. Overall, this is a great area for outdoor sports throughout the year.
- Website: **www.Schloss-Lichtenstein.de**

Hohenneuffen Castle (Burg Hohenneuffen): This castle differs dramatically from the previously described Lichtenstein and Hohenzollern castles. Burg Hohenneuffen is largely in ruin while the other two are well preserved with many rooms to visit and explore.

Hohenneuffen Castle
Intriguing Castle Ruins to Explore.
Photo source: Wikimedia Commons

There is an interesting mix here of a large ruin with an enjoyable restaurant sitting in the middle courtyard. This is a large castle complex with a history dating to the 12th century. It had served as a fortress in the 16th century and was used as a stronghold to defend the Württemberg state. Despite the ruined state, coming here is educational and worth the trip. The ruins are expansive with much to explore and the views of the Black Forest and valleys in every direction are tremendous.

One caution, the primary parking lot sits below the castle which necessitates a lengthy uphill trek to the castle and its restaurant.

- Entry Fee: Courtyard & grounds – no fee. Guided walks – adults 5 € / Children 2,50€. Falconry demonstration 5 € for adults.

- **Location**: Above the town of Neffen. A 45-minute drive south from Stuttgart. The first part of the trip is on a highway with the last portion along a back road.

- **Address**: Hohenneuffen, 72629 Neuffen

- **How to Get Here:** The best way to travel is by car. A train-bus combination is available but takes about 2 hours in each direction. Trains may be taken to the town of Neuffen which sits at the base of the hill below the castle. From there, a bus or a 30-minute hike is necessary. Once at the castle, there is paid parking near the castle. Caution: There is a steep walk uphill to the castle from the primary parking lot. An alternate lot is available close to the castle for individuals with limited mobility.

- **Facilities**: Toilets and a kiosk in the courtyard serving local Swabian snacks. A full-service restaurant is open for special events and group gatherings. Several guided tours are available.

- **Hours**: Hours do vary by season, but typical hours are from 9 AM to 5 PM. In the summer, the closing hours for most days are 7 PM. Open every day except some holidays.

- **Tours from Stuttgart**: No structured group tours are available from Stuttgart.

- **Nearby:** This castle is on an isolated hilltop and there is nothing else in the way of facilities here. Numerous and expansive trails are available. This is a popular area for hiking and winter sports. In the valley below are thermal baths, the "Panorama Therme Beuren."

- **Websites:** Castle: **www.Festungsruine-Hohenneuffen.de** / Restaurant: **www.Hohenneuffen.de**

Other Palaces & Castles in the Area:[13] The three castles described in the previous pages are far from the only ones in the area. Many other palaces and castles are nearby. Some, unfortunately, may only be viewed from outside while others provide full tours. Examples of other castles to explore follow.

Heidelberg Castle / Schloss Heidelberg. Beautiful 13th century hilltop castle situated above the city of Heidelberg. Rebuilt in 1900. A mix of ruins and reconstructed sections.

Heidelberg Castle / Schloss Heidelberg
Photo source: R. Wolf - Wikimedia Commons

- Traveling to Heidelberg from Stuttgart: This is a 50-minute train ride or 90-minute drive northwest from Stuttgart. See the next chapter on Day Trips for further information on

---

[13] **Visiting Neuschwanstein:** The country's most popular castle, which has similarity to Hohenzollern-Sigmaringen, is Neuschwanstein. Do not attempt to take a day trip to Neuschwanstein from Stuttgart as it is roughly a 2 ½ hour drive each way. When staying in Stuttgart, focus on the magnificent castles which are much easier to reach and not as crowded.

Heidelberg. Taking a train necessitates switching to a bus or tram once in Heidelberg to get up to the castle.

- Website: **www.Schloss-Heidelberg.de**

Karlsruhe Palace. Located in the town of Karlsruhe along the Rhine River, Karlsruhe Palace is another "Versailles-like" palace with numerous ornate rooms and impressive formal gardens. The palace complex is located near the center of town and has local markets and shops nearby.

- Traveling from Stuttgart: This is a 55-minute trip from Stuttgart by train or car. Numerous trains make the trip each day, making this an easy destination travel to.
- Website: **www.LandesMuseum.de**

Ludwigsburg Residential Palace: One of 3 palaces in Ludwigsburg. This is an expansive, baroque palace and complex and has justifiably been nicknamed "The Versailles of Swabia." Guided tours are available although they are primarily in German. The palace was the royal seat of power in the 18th century.

Ludwigsburg Residential Palace & Gardens

- Traveling from Stuttgart: An easy 10-minute S-Bahn trip to Ludwigsburg then a 15-minute walk or short bus ride to the palace.
- Website: **www.Schloss-Ludwigsburg.de**

Schloss Favorite. Another palace in Ludwigsburg. This is a fully refurbished palace with extensive grounds and gardens to explore. It is within walking distance to Ludwigsburg Residential Palace and the two combined make a full day of exploring.

- Traveling from Stuttgart: There are several options for travel. A car is best as it will take you directly to the palace. Another option is to take the S-Bahn to the Favorite Park station then walk 20 minutes from there.
- Website: **www.Schloss-Favorite-Ludwigsburg.de**

Schloss Favorite - Ludwigsburg

Exploring the towns and cities around Stuttgart is fun and can provide a great opportunity to experience portions of Germany which provide very different experiences from modern-day Stuttgart.

This guide does not list every place you could visit near Stuttgart. The focus here is on a selection of "reachable" and delightful destinations by train or car and on trips which can be done in one day without wearing yourself down. Check out the map and graph on the following pages for likely travel times and distances to select towns from Stuttgart.

Five destinations are described in this chapter. These are far from the only enjoyable destinations in the area, but they each provide a different atmosphere and set of experiences.

Each of the towns listed here can easily be reached by train and or car and meet the criteria of being less than 90-minutes each way from Stuttgart and provide a variety of interesting sights along with pleasant strolling. All towns outlined here also have easy access to a central train station.

> Each of the destinations outlined here may be visited by train or bus. Cars are not required.

---

[14] **Nearby Major Cities:** Cities such as Frankfurt and Nuremberg are not included here as these cities generally require much more than a simple day trip even though they can be traveled to/from Stuttgart within a day.

Suggested Day Trips from Stuttgart

Recommended castle visits are listed in Chapter 9.

Germany Town	Popu-lation	Driving Time from central Stuttgart	Travel Time by Train
Bad Wildbad	10,000	1hr & 10min	1hr 10min
Baden-Baden	55,000	1hr & 15min	1hr & 15min+
Esslingen	93,000	15-to-20min	10 min
Heidelberg	160,000	1hr & 20min	40 min
Tübingen	90,000	40 min	45 min

Bad Wildbad: There is something for everyone in this resort destination. Bad Wildbad (Wild Bath in English) is not only a beautiful town in the Black Forest, but also a nature-lovers dream.

This is a charming town located in a deep river valley. A picturesque lane along the river Enz is lined with shops and restaurants. Looking upward from the town are steep, forested hillsides. There are two distinct areas to this town of 10,000: the town with its shops, parks and restaurants, and the plateau above with its focus on outdoor enjoyment.

Bad Wildbad Town Center

Bad Wildbad is a popular vacation spot due to its beautiful setting and numerous opportunities to enjoy the outdoors and natural delights such as hot springs. For the more culturally minded, there is an outdoor theater which is largely devoted to opera.

Reaching up westward from a location near the train station is a funicular that takes riders up to a wooded plateau which provides an extensive array of activities for visitors. Even if you do not wish to participate in any of the attractions at the top of the hill, this trip should be considered as it provides great views of the town and valley.

With all of the activities available, you may want to consider spending one or more nights here. There are numerous hotels and spa-hotels to select from. A detailed list may be found on the city's website at: **www.Bad-Wildbad.de**

Bad Wildbad Highlights:

- **Treetop Walk** (Baumwipfelpfad Schwarzwald): Located on the hilltop above Bad Wildbad is a unique tower which rises over 60 meters (almost 200 feet) above the forest floor. At the top, there are unobstructed views of the Black Forest in all directions. For some added fun, there is a circular slide which you can choose for an exhilarating ride down. The website for this attraction is the same one for the funicular railway.

The "Treetop Walk" in Bad Wildbad
(Baumwipfelpfad Schwarzwald)

- **Sommerberg Funicular Railway:** The highest funicular in the Baden-Württemberg area. It rises 300 meters above the

town below and connects Bad Wildbad with the Sommerberg area which is an extensive outdoor recreation area. The lower station is near the center of town and only a block from the train station. For full details and current rates, check the website at: **www.Baumwipfelpfade.de.**

- Wildline Hangbrucke: Located near the funicular railway and Treetop Walk is a long suspension bridge which spans 380 meters, (over 1,200 feet or almost ¼ mile). There is a fee of 9€ to cross this bridge, but it is worth it as the views and experience are quite enjoyable. The website for this bridge is: **www.Wildline.de.**

- Thermal Baths: In the town of Bad-Wildbad, there are two popular thermal baths which take advantage of the local hot springs. Both are spas, but you may also simply come in to relax and enjoy the hot mineral baths. The two spas are Palais Thermal and Vital Therme. Information on both locations may be found in the visitor's office website at: **www.Bad-Wildbad.de/thermen-schwarzwald.**

Traveling to Bad Wildbad:

- Train: A train trip from Stuttgart takes 1 hour and 10 minutes. The train station in Bad Wildbad is in the central part of town and convenient for attractions.

- Driving: A drive from central Stuttgart takes one hour. Parking right in town is scarce and it is often necessary to select a lot near the northern end of town.

Baden-Baden, Germany: This small city of fifty-five thousand sits in a valley near the Rhine River and is nestled in the northern foothills of the Black Forest. It is largely known as being a spa town associated with the rich and famous.

Baden-Baden

The town gets its name from the warm springs and historic Roman baths found here. It was developed as a spa starting in the early 1800's.

The word "Baden" means bath but became the expanded name of "Baden-Baden" as there were other towns with the name of Baden. To clarify the location, the name became "Baden in Baden" which was later shortened to Baden-Baden.

The city's website provides a good overview of the numerous sights to see along with helpful information on parking and getting around town. **www.Baden-Baden.com.**

<u>Getting Around in Baden-Baden:</u> Most of what you will want to do can be accomplished by simply walking around. A small city train, the "City-Bahn," operates Spring thru Fall and will take you to most major stops. The price per adult for a day ticket is around 7,5€. The complete circuit takes a bit under an hour.

A fun, although expensive, alternative is to ride one of the numerous horse-drawn carriages. Expect to pay around 120€ (plus tip) for a one-hour tour. These are readily available in the historic district.

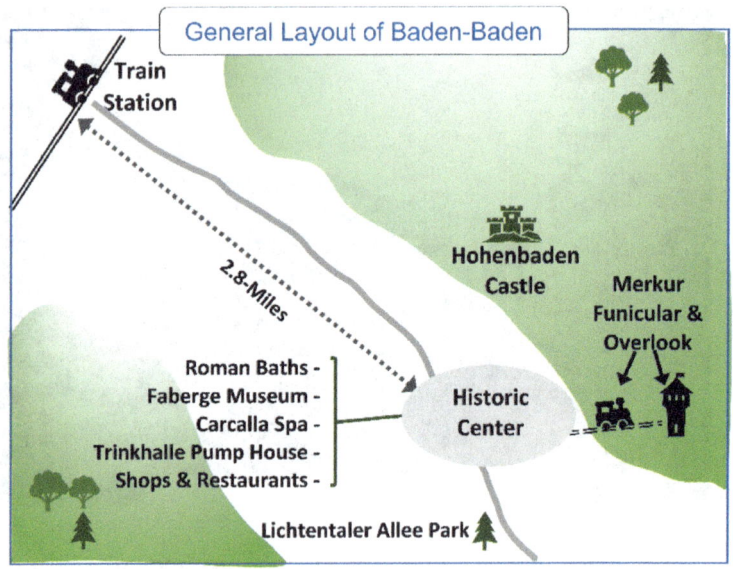

Baden-Baden Highlights:

- Original Roman Baths: This is a "do not miss" attraction. The 2,000-year-old Roman Bath ruins are a short 5 to 8-minute walk from the bus stop where you can view this ancient facility.

- Historic Old Town: Stroll the long pedestrian streets lined with upscale shopping. Find a restaurant and enjoy some delicious Black Forest Cake.

- Fabergé Museum: Located near the old town, this museum is devoted specifically to the works of Fabergé. Items on display include eggs and jewelry once owned by the Russian Tsars.

- Caracalla Spa: With any luck, you will have packed bathing suits so you can take a dip in this historic and elegant hot mineral bath. The building is close to the Roman Baths and offers both indoor and outdoor pools.

- Hohenbaden Castle: An ancient fortress which is partially in ruins. It is situated on a hillside overlooking the town and provides excellent views. It can be a bit of an arduous walk uphill to reach it.

- Merkur Mountain Funicular: Take an enjoyable funicular ride up to the highest point in Baden-Baden. Until recently, this was the steepest funicular in Europe. For a relaxing day, consider riding up and walking back down. The views from here enable you to see much of the valley below.

- Horse and Carriage Tours: The horse and carriage tours are a relaxing way to tour the sights. Two versions are available, but the longer 1-hour tour will give you a fuller tour of this quaint city.

How to get to Baden-Baden from Stuttgart:

- Train: The train from Stuttgart will take up to 90 minutes, depending on which train you select. When you arrive in Baden-Baden, the train station is over two miles from the central historic and tourist area.

  Do not attempt to walk into town from the train station as the walk has heavy traffic along the way. Take a bus into town from the train station. The buses will be clearly marked. Look for the "Leopoldsplatz" bus #205 which takes you directly to the center of town. Cost for the bus is approximately €2 and travel time is around 15 minutes. Once you depart the bus, there is an impressive array of shops and restaurants just a few feet away.

- Driving: Travel time by car is similar to taking the train and will be around one-hour and 15-minutes. A parking garage is available near the center of town.

Esslingen, Germany (Esslingen am Neckar): A short distance south on the Neckar River from Stuttgart is Esslingen, a city with appealing half-timbered, colorful houses. Esslingen remarkably escaped the heaving bombing which destroyed much of nearby Stuttgart.

Esslingen, Germany (Esslingen am Neckar)
Charming small city along the Neckar River

This is a relaxing half-day trip with the old town serving as the focal point. If you are lucky to be in the area at Christmas, be sure to check out the medieval Christmas Market which lasts nearly four weeks each year.

The central highlight is the town itself with its many historical buildings. Sitting above the town is an expansive fortress with town walls and there are vineyards which can easily be explored on foot.

Esslingen Highlights:

- **Esslingen Burg:** This ancient fortress is the most popular and notable attraction in Esslingen. Built in the 14th century, it was built to protect the town and area. The complex includes high walls and battlements. After a noteworthy uphill walk, you can explore the grounds and enjoy excellent views of the town

- Wine Walk: Each Spring, the area's wine growers encourage visitors to stroll from the town into the vineyards and, with glass in hand, sample local wines.

- Old Town Buildings: Several buildings of note can be found in the heart of town, and several are open to visitors. These include:

  o Kessler Sekt – wine cellar and tasting room.

  o Altes Rathaus: This ancient town hall with carillon bells is one of the most photographed buildings in the area.

  o Esslinger Stadtkirche St. Dionys: 14th century church in the heart of town. Under the church, is an extensive crypt which can be explored.

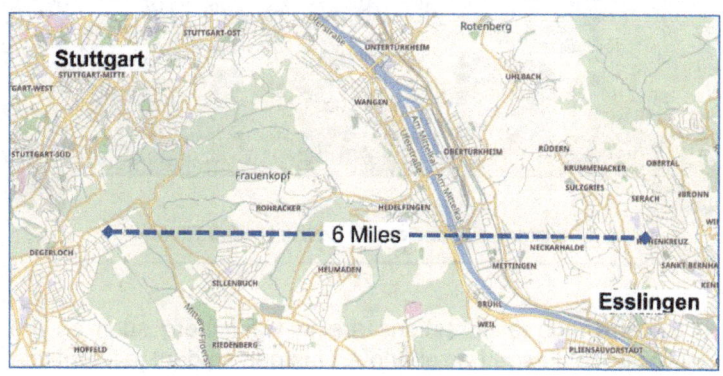

How to get to Esslingen:

- Train: The train from Stuttgart to Esslingen (the train station is cited as "Esslingen am Neckar") takes only 10 minutes. There are several train choices including the light-rail S-1 line. The station is immediately next to the central town with its numerous shops and sights.

- Car: Driving from central Stuttgart takes roughly 20 minutes and parking is generally not problematic.

Heidelberg, Germany: With a population of 160,000, Heidelberg is the largest of the six towns recommended in this guide and can justify a guidebook of its own. This noted college town is located on the Neckar River (the same river which flows through Stuttgart). Much of the town sits in a river valley with high hills and forests bordering the city.

Heidelberg, Germany
Historic city and castle on the Neckar River

Several unique attractions are in Heidelberg such as the world's largest wine barrel and an historic student jail. Outside of the historic Old Town, some attractions, such as the zoo, are not within walking distance, so using the local transportation system of trams and buses can be beneficial.

The city's website provides details on the numerous sights to see along with helpful information on parking and getting around town. www.Tourism-Heidelberg.com. With the numerous historical buildings in Old Town, consider signing up for one of the walking tours. A good source for this is Henry Heidelberg Tours at www.HenryHeidelbergTours.com

Getting around in Heidelberg: For a small city, Heidelberg has an impressive transportation system, and the buses and tram system is popular. A great way to get to the western edge of Old Town from the main train station is by tram. Maps of the local transportation are found at most stops along with ticket machines which provide an English option. Trams do not go into the heart of Old Town, but buses do.

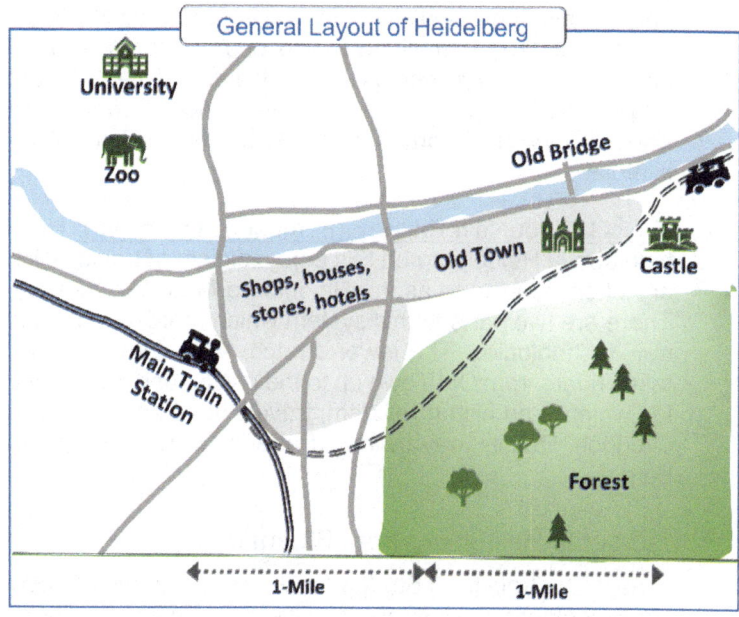

A day pass can be purchased which includes unlimited trips. This can be helpful if you will be traveling to the university or zoo. Taxis are also typically available and can generally be found at the main train station.

Heidelberg Highlights:

- Heidelberg Castle: The expansive ruins of a Renaissance-era castle and Heidelberg's main attraction outside of Old Town. The castle sits 300feet above Heidelberg, providing exceptional views of the city below. This is a complex of buildings and were built in different eras with differing styles. Portions of the castle have been rebuilt providing the ability to explore the world's largest wine barrel and an apothecary museum. The best way to reach the castle is via a funicular which leads from old town.

- Old Town (Altstadt): For most visitors to Heidelberg, this area will be the focal point of the visit. Altstadt is the oldest part of Heidelberg and sits below an imposing castle. It is a pleasant maze of small lanes and open squares. A great place to start exploring is Bismarkplatz on the western edge. Popular sites include: The Market Square, Old Bridge, Town Hall, Korn Market, and Student Jail at Universitätplatz.

- Funicular/Mountain Railway (Bergbahn-Heidelberg): Head high above Heidelberg on this enjoyable set of trains which are often referred to as the Heidelberg Mountain Railway. There are two parts to this system which represent old and new technologies. The lower stretch, a modern funicular, takes riders from Old Town up to the castle, and the second leg which is an historic system, travels up to an impressive overlook. Details may be found at www.Bergbahn-Heidelberg.de.

How to get to Heidelberg from Stuttgart:

- Train: The train from Stuttgart is the fastest mode of travel to Heidelberg. Trains take as little as 40 minutes. These trains will take you to the main station at "Heidelberg-Hauptbahhof." Another smaller station, "Heidelberg-Altstadt," takes riders to a small station on the east side of old town. To do this, a change of trains at the main station is required.

  It is a long walk, about 30-to-40 minutes to the center of Old Town from the train station. To avoid this, consider taking a taxi or a tram to Bismarckplatz to begin your explorations.

- Driving: Travel time by car is longer than the train, but you can drive directly to Old Town and park in one of the lots there.

Tübingen, Germany: Imagine a delightful, colorful labyrinth of half-timbered homes, many of which overlook the Neckar River, and this is the town of Tübingen. Like Heidelberg, this is a vibrant college town of 90,000 with nearly one-third of the population being students. Due to the influx of college students, Tübingen has the lowest median age of any city in Germany.

Tübingen, Germany

Limited Mobility Caution

Tübingen has some steep walks and many cobblestone streets which can be a challenge for individuals with mobility limitations.

The town is an enjoyable mixture of cobblestone lanes and small plazas. Numerous historic buildings and outdoor restaurants line the streets and plazas. Architecture is a mix of Renaissance and Medieval periods with few modern structures in between. When here, consider taking a walking tour with a local guide as many of the structures have long histories. Information on walking tours may be found at **www.Tuebingen-info.de.**

Given the youthful vibrance here, there is no shortage of wine cellars and beer gardens. Multiple large beer gardens/halls line the river, providing for a great view.

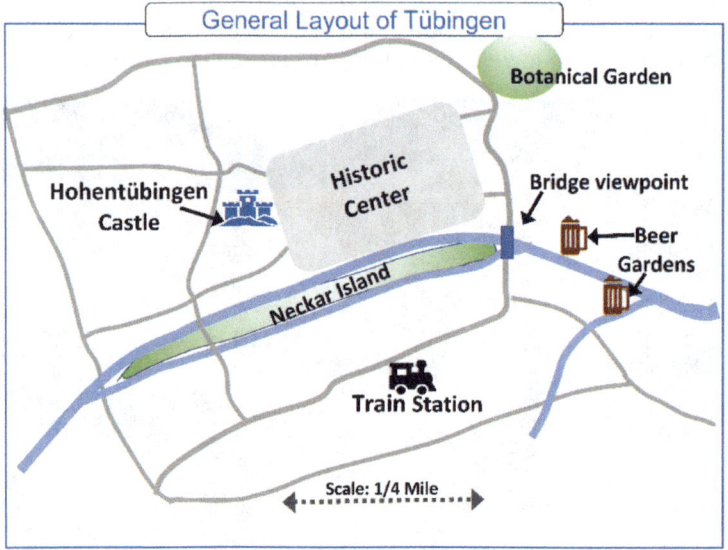

Tübingen Highlights:

- **Tübingen's Old Town:** An enjoyable set of narrow streets, restaurants, and historical places including: Marktplatz, The Rathaus, old government offices, the Stadtmuseum, and more. Bring a camera as this is a very photogenic town.

- **Hohentübingen Castle:** A well-preserved castle built in the 11th through 16th century which looks over the town. It is a bit of an uphill walk to reach the castle, but the complex is large and worth exploring.

- **Punting on the river:** Punts are small, flat boats which are maneuvered by poles. These boats are available for rent or group tours on the Neckar River which sits along the town's historic center. A lot of fun and some laughs. Details may be found at www.Tuebingen.de.

- **Beer Gardens:** You are in Germany, and this is a college town. Put the two together and this equals beer, lots of it. You will find several fun beer gardens. Two of the larger ones overlook the Neckar River.

- **Neckarinsel Park:** A long, narrow island on the Neckar River, just below the town center, contains an impressive park. It was planted hundreds of years ago and there are relaxing walkways through rows of trees along with several sculptures.

- **Botanical Garden:** A short stroll north of the center of town is a very large botanical garden, the "Botanischer Garten." Like many other aspects of this town, such as the punting rides, this is owned and managed by the university.

How to get to Tübingen:

- **Train:** Trains from Stuttgart will take around 45 minutes each way. It is necessary to start the journey from Stuttgart's main station as the S-Bahn does not service Tübingen.

  There is a walk of approximately 15 minutes into town. If your time and abilities allow, take this walk. It is both pleasant and provides great views, especially when crossing the main bridge, the "Eberhardsbrücke." In addition, the town's tourist office is next to the bridge and the staff here can provide valuable guidance and information on local tours.

- **Driving:** Travel time by car is around 40 minutes and parking lots in Tübingen are generally easy to find. Bringing a car provides the bonus of being able to visit the nearby castles of Lichtenstein or Hohenzollern while in the area.

Index

Starting-Point Guides

This guidebook on Stuttgart is one of several current and planned *Starting-Point Guides*. Each book in the series is developed with the concept of using one enjoyable city as your basecamp and then exploring from there.

Current guidebooks are for:

Austria:

- Salzburg, and the Salzburg area.

France:

- Bordeaux, Plus the surrounding Gironde River region
- Dijon Plus the Burgundy Region
- Lille and the Nord-Pas-de-Calais Area.
- Lyon, Plus the Saône and Rhône Confluence Region
- Nantes and the western Loire Valley.
- Reims and Épernay the heart of the Champagne Region.
- Strasbourg, and the central Alsace region.
- Toulouse, and the Haute-Garonne area.

Germany:

- Cologne & Bonn
- Dresden and the Saxony State
- Stuttgart and the and the Baden-Württemberg area.

Spain:

- <u>Camino Easy</u>: A mature walker's guide to the popular Camino de Santiago trail.
- <u>Toledo:</u> The City of Three Cultures

Sweden:

- <u>Gothenburg</u> Plus the Västra Götaland region.

Switzerland:

- <u>Geneva</u>, Including the Lake Geneva area.
- <u>Lucerne</u>, Including the Lake Lucerne area.
- <u>Zurich</u> – And the Lake Zurich area.

Updates on these and other titles may be found on the author's Facebook page at:

www.Facebook.com/BGPreston.author

Feel free to use this Facebook page to provide feedback and suggestions to the author or email to: cincy3@gmail.com

Made in the USA
Las Vegas, NV
09 July 2024

92064697R10075